FAREWELL
ADDRESSES
of the
Presidents
of the United States

—★—

FAREWELL ADDRESSES

of the
Presidents
of the United States

———★———

APPLEWOOD BOOKS
Publishers of America's Living Past
Carlisle, Massachusetts

ISBN 978-1-4290-9443-6

MANUFACTURED IN
THE UNITED STATES OF AMERICA

TABLE OF CONTENTS

GEORGE WASHINGTON - Farewell Address (1796).....................Page 7

ANDREW JACKSON - Farewell Address (1837).....................................21

ANDREW JOHNSON - Farewell Address (1869)................................. 39

HARRY S. TRUMAN - Farewell Address (1953)................................. 49

DWIGHT D. EISENHOWER - Farewell Address (1961).........................59

JIMMY CARTER - Farewell Address (1981)... 65

RONALD REAGAN - Farewell Address (1989).......................................71

WILLIAM JEFFERSON CLINTON - Farewell Address (2001)............. 79

GEORGE W. BUSH - Farewell Address (2009)....................................... 83

BARACK H. OBAMA - Farewell Address (2017) 89

FOREWORD

FROM GEORGE WASHINGTON TO BARACK OBAMA, presidential farewell addresses have served, on the one hand, as a vehicle for a departing chief executive to use the accumulated wisdom of a presidency to look forward in time and see opportunity and danger in an American future, and, on the other hand, as a way to look back on his presidency and suggest how it should be seen by future generations.

George Washington's farewell address, directed to "Friends and Fellow-Citizens" and published in a Philadelphia newspaper in 1796, set the standard. Each year since 1896, on February 22, Washington's birthday, George Washington's farewell address has been read in the Senate by a senator. Washington's message to the future—to leave our party affiliations aside, avoid geographical sectionalism, and protect the stability of our nation from interference by foreign powers—has been good advice to presidents from John Adams to Donald J. Trump. In 1956, Minnesota Senator Hubert Humphrey wrote that every American should have a chance to read Washington's address: "It gives one a renewed sense of pride in our republic."

Reading these addresses is like opening a time capsule. Each is a reminder of how much we, as a nation, have changed and how much we have stayed the same.

George Washington

FAREWELL ADDRESS
MONDAY, SEPTEMBER 19, 1796

President Washington's farewell address was first printed in the Philadelphia newspaper American Daily Advertiser *on September 19, 1796. James Madison wrote parts of the introduction a few years earlier in 1792, and Alexander Hamilton helped edit Washington's draft for the 1796 address. Washington's address set the tone for all future presidential farewell addresses.*

Friends and Fellow-Citizens:

THE PERIOD FOR A NEW ELECTION of a citizen to administer the Executive Government of the United States being not far distant, and the time actually arrived when your thoughts must be employed in designating the person who is to be clothed with that important trust, it appears to me proper, especially as it may conduce to a more distinct expression of the public voice, that I should now apprise you of the resolution I have formed to decline being considered among the number of those out of whom a choice is to be made.

I beg you at the same time to do me the justice to be assured that this resolution has not been taken without a strict regard to all the considerations appertaining to the relation which binds a dutiful citizen to his country; and that in withdrawing the tender of service, which silence in my Situation might imply, I am influenced by no diminution of zeal for your future interest, no deficiency of grateful respect for your past kindness, but am supported by a full conviction that the step is compatible with both.

The acceptance of and continuance hitherto in the office to which your suffrages have twice called me have been a uniform sacrifice of inclination to the opinion of duty and to a deference for what appeared to be your desire. I constantly hoped that it would have been much earlier in my power, consistently with motives which I was not at liberty to disregard, to return to that retirement from which I had been reluctantly drawn. The strength of my inclination to do this previous to the last election had even led to the preparation of an address to declare it to you; but mature reflection on the then perplexed and critical posture of our affairs with foreign nations and the unanimous advice of persons entitled to my confidence impelled me to abandon the idea. I rejoice that the state of your concerns, external as well as internal, no longer renders the pursuit of inclination incompatible with the sentiment of duty or propriety, and am persuaded, whatever partiality may be retained for my services, that in the present circumstances of our country you will not disapprove my determination to retire.

The impressions with which I first undertook the arduous trust were explained on the proper occasion. In the discharge of this trust I will only say that I have, with good intentions, contributed toward the organization and administration of the Government the best exertions of which a very fallible judgment was capable. Not unconscious in the outset of the inferiority of my qualifications, experience in my own eyes, perhaps still more in the eyes of others, has strengthened the motives to diffidence of myself; and every day the increasing weight of years admonishes me more and more that the shade of retirement is as necessary to me as it will be welcome. Satisfied that if any circumstances have given peculiar value to my services they were temporary, I have the consolation to believe that, while choice and prudence invite me to quit the political scene, patriotism does not forbid it.

In looking forward to the moment which is intended to terminate the career of my political life my feelings do not permit me to suspend the deep acknowledgment of that debt of gratitude which I owe to my beloved country for the many honors it has conferred upon me; still more for the steadfast confidence with which it has supported me, and for the opportunities I have thence enjoyed of manifesting my inviolable attachment by services faithful and persevering, though in usefulness unequal to my zeal. If benefits have resulted to our country from these services, let it always be remembered to your praise and as an instructive example in our annals that under circumstances in which the passions, agitated in every direction, were liable to mislead; amidst appearances sometimes dubious; vicissitudes of fortune often discouraging; in situations in which not unfrequently want of success has countenanced the spirit of criticism, the constancy of your support was the essential prop of the efforts and a guaranty of the plans by which they were effected. Profoundly penetrated with this idea, I shall carry it with me to my grave as a strong incitement to unceasing vows that Heaven may continue to you the choicest tokens of its beneficence; that your union and brotherly affection may be perpetual; that the free Constitution which is the work of your hands may be sacredly maintained; that its administration in every department may be stamped with wisdom and virtue; that, in fine, the happiness of the people of these States, under the auspices of liberty, may be made complete by so careful a preservation and so prudent a use of this blessing as will acquire to them the glory of recommending it to the applause, the affection, and adoption of every nation which is yet a stranger to it.

Here, perhaps, I ought to stop. But a solicitude for your welfare which can not end but with my life, and the apprehension of danger natural to that solicitude, urge me on an occasion like the present to offer to your solemn contemplation and to recommend to your frequent review some sentiments which are the result of much reflection, of no inconsiderable observation, and which appear to me all important to the permanency of your felicity as a people. These will be offered to you with the more freedom as you can only see in them the disinterested warnings of a parting friend, who can possibly have no personal motive to bias his counsel. Nor can I forget as an encouragement to it your indulgent reception of my sentiments on a former and not dissimilar occasion.

Interwoven as is the love of liberty with every ligament of your hearts, no recommendation of mine is necessary to fortify or confirm the attachment.

The unity of government which constitutes you one people is also now dear to you. It is justly so, for it is a main pillar in the edifice of your real independence, the support of your tranquillity at home, your peace abroad, of your safety, of your prosperity, of that very liberty which you so highly prize. But as it is easy to foresee that from different causes and from different quarters much pains will be taken, many artifices employed, to weaken in your minds the conviction of this truth, as this is the point in your political fortress against which the batteries of internal and external enemies will be most constantly and actively (though often covertly and insidiously) directed, it is of infinite moment that you should properly estimate the immense value of your national union to your collective and individual happiness; that you should cherish a cordial, habitual, and immovable attachment to it; accustoming yourselves to think and speak of it as of the palladium of your political safety and prosperity; watching for its preservation with jealous anxiety; discountenancing whatever may suggest even a suspicion that it can in any event be abandoned, and indignantly frowning upon the first dawning of every attempt to alienate any portion of our country from the rest or to enfeeble the sacred ties which now link together the various parts.

For this you have every inducement of sympathy and interest. Citizens by birth or choice of a common country, that country has a right to concentrate your affections. The name of American, which belongs to you in your national capacity, must always exalt the just pride of patriotism more than any appellation derived from local discriminations. With slight shades of difference, you have the same religion, manners, habits, and political principles. You have in a common cause fought and triumphed together. The independence and liberty you possess are the work of joint councils and joint efforts, of common dangers, sufferings, and successes.

But these considerations, however powerfully they address themselves to your sensibility, are greatly outweighed by those which apply more immediately to your interest. Here every portion of our country finds the most commanding motives for carefully guarding and preserving the union of the whole.

The North, in an unrestrained intercourse with the South, protected by the equal laws of a common government, finds in the productions of the latter great additional resources of maritime and commercial enterprise and precious materials of manufacturing industry. The South, in the same intercourse, benefiting by the same agency of the North, sees its agriculture grow and its commerce expand. Turning partly into its own channels the seamen of the North, it finds its particular navigation invigorated; and while it contributes in different ways to nourish and increase the general mass of the national navigation, it looks forward to the protection of a maritime strength to which itself is unequally adapted. The East, in a like intercourse with the West, already finds, and in the progressive improvement of interior communications by land and water will more and more find, a valuable vent for the commodities which it brings from abroad or manufactures at home. The West derives from the East supplies requisite to its growth and comfort, and what is perhaps of still greater consequence, it must of necessity owe the secure enjoyment of indispensable outlets for its own productions to the weight, influence, and the future maritime strength of the Atlantic side of the Union, directed by an indissoluble community of interest as one nation. Any other tenure by which the West can hold this essential advantage, whether derived from its own separate strength or from an apostate and unnatural connection with any foreign power, must be intrinsically precarious.

While, then, every part of our country thus feels an immediate and particular interest in union, all the parts combined can not fail to find in the united mass of means and efforts greater strength, greater resource, proportionably greater security from external danger, a less frequent interruption of their peace by foreign nations, and what is of inestimable value, they must derive from union an exemption from those broils and wars between themselves which so frequently afflict neighboring countries not tied together by the same governments, which their own rivalships alone would be sufficient to produce, but which opposite foreign alliances, attachments, and intrigues would stimulate and imbitter. Hence, likewise, they will avoid the necessity of those overgrown military establishments which, under any form of government, are inauspicious to liberty, and which are to be regarded as particularly hostile to republican liberty. In this sense it is that your union ought to be considered as a main prop of your liberty, and that the love of the one ought to endear to you the preservation of the other.

These considerations speak a persuasive language to every reflecting and virtuous mind, and exhibit the continuance of the union as a primary object of patriotic desire. Is there a doubt whether a common government can embrace so large a sphere? Let experience solve it. To listen to mere speculation in such a case were criminal. We are authorized to hope that a proper organization of the whole, with the auxiliary agency of governments for the respective subdivisions, will afford a happy issue to the experiment. It is well worth a fair and full experiment. With such powerful and obvious motives to union affecting all parts of our country, while experience shall not have demonstrated its impracticability, there will always be reason to distrust the patriotism of those who in any quarter may endeavor to weaken its bands.

In contemplating the causes which may disturb our union it occurs as matter of serious concern that any ground should have been furnished for characterizing parties by geographical discriminations—Northern and Southern, Atlantic and Western—whence designing men may endeavor to excite a belief that there is a real difference of local interests and views. One of the expedients of party to acquire influence within particular districts is to misrepresent the opinions and aims of other districts. You can not shield yourselves too much against the jealousies and heartburnings which spring from these misrepresentations; they tend to render alien to each other those who ought to be bound together by fraternal affection. The inhabitants of our Western country have lately had a useful lesson on this head. They have seen in the negotiation by the Executive and in the unanimous ratification by the Senate of the treaty with Spain, and in the universal satisfaction at that event throughout the United States, a decisive proof how unfounded were the suspicions propagated among them of a policy in the General Government and in the Atlantic States unfriendly to their interests in regard to the Mississippi. They have been witnesses to the formation of two treaties that with Great Britain and that with Spain—which secure to them everything they could desire in respect to our foreign relations toward confirming their prosperity. Will it not be their wisdom to rely for the preservation of these advantages on the union by which they were procured? Will they not henceforth be deaf to those advisers, if such there are, who would sever them from their brethren and connect them with aliens?

To the efficacy and permanency of your union a government for the whole is indispensable. No alliances, however strict, between the parts can be an adequate substitute. They must inevitably experience the infractions and interruptions which all alliances in all times have experienced. Sensible of this momentous truth, you have improved upon your first essay by the adoption of a Constitution of Government better calculated than your former for an intimate union and for the efficacious management of your common concerns. This Government, the offspring of our own choice, uninfluenced and unawed, adopted upon full investigation and mature deliberation, completely free in its principles, in the distribution of its powers, uniting security with energy, and containing within itself a provision for its own amendment, has a just claim to your confidence and your support. Respect for its authority, compliance with its laws, acquiescence in its measures, are duties enjoined by the fundamental maxims of true liberty. The basis of our political systems is the right of the people to make and to alter their constitutions of government. But the constitution which at any time exists till changed by an explicit and authentic act of the whole people is sacredly obligatory upon all. The very idea of the power and the right of the people to establish government presupposes the duty of every individual to obey the established government.

All obstructions to the execution of the laws, all combinations and associations, under whatever plausible character, with the real design to direct, control, counteract, or awe the regular deliberation and action of the constituted authorities, are destructive of this fundamental principle and of fatal tendency. They serve to organize faction; to give it an artificial and extraordinary force; to put in the place of the delegated will of the nation the will of a party, often a small but artful and enterprising minority of the community, and, according to the alternate triumphs of different parties, to make the public administration the mirror of the ill-concerted and incongruous projects of faction rather than the organ of consistent and wholesome plans, digested by common counsels and modified by mutual interests.

However combinations or associations of the above description may now and then answer popular ends, they are likely in the course of time and things to become potent engines by which cunning, ambitious, and unprincipled men will be enabled to subvert the power of the people, and to usurp for themselves the reins of government, destroying afterwards the very engines which have lifted them to unjust dominion.

Toward the preservation of your Government and the permanency of your present happy state, it is requisite not only that you steadily discountenance irregular oppositions to its acknowledged authority, but also that you resist with care the spirit of innovation upon its principles, however specious the pretexts. One method of assault may be to effect in the forms of the Constitution alterations which will impair the energy of the system, and thus to undermine what can not be directly overthrown. In all the changes to which you may be invited remember that time and habit are at least as necessary to fix the true character of governments as of other human institutions; that experience is the surest standard by which to test the real tendency of the existing constitution of a country; that facility in changes upon the credit of mere hypothesis and opinion exposes to perpetual change, from the endless variety of hypothesis and opinion; and remember especially that for the efficient management of your common interests in a country so extensive as ours a government of as much vigor as is consistent with the perfect security of liberty is indispensable. Liberty itself will find in such a government, with powers properly distributed and adjusted, its surest guardian. It is, indeed, little else than a name where the government is too feeble to withstand the enterprises of faction, to confine each member of the society within the limits prescribed by the laws, and to maintain all in the secure and tranquil enjoyment of the rights of person and property.

I have already intimated to you the danger of parties in the State, with particular reference to the founding of them on geographical discriminations. Let me now take a more comprehensive view, and warn you in the most solemn manner against the baneful effects of the spirit of party generally.

This spirit, unfortunately, is inseparable from our nature, having its root in the strongest passions of the human mind. It exists under different shapes in all governments, more or less stifled, controlled, or repressed; but in those of the popular form it is seen in its greatest rankness and is truly their worst enemy.

The alternate domination of one faction over another, sharpened by the spirit of revenge natural to party dissension, which in different ages and countries has perpetrated the most horrid enormities, is itself a frightful despotism. But this leads at length to a more formal and permanent despotism. The disorders and miseries which result gradually incline the minds of men to seek security and repose in the absolute power of an individual, and sooner or later the chief of some prevailing faction, more able or more fortunate than his competitors, turns this disposition to the purposes of his own elevation on the ruins of public liberty.

Without looking forward to an extremity of this kind (which nevertheless ought not to be entirely out of sight), the common and continual mischiefs of the spirit of party are sufficient to make it the interest and duty of a wise people to discourage and restrain it.

It serves always to distract the public councils and enfeeble the public administration. It agitates the community with ill-rounded jealousies and false alarms; kindles the animosity of one part against another; foments occasionally riot and insurrection. It opens the door to foreign influence and corruption, which find a facilitated access to the government itself through the channels of party passion. Thus the policy and the will of one country are subjected to the policy and will of another.

There is an opinion that parties in free countries are useful checks upon the administration of the government, and serve to keep alive the spirit of liberty. This within certain limits is probably true; and in governments of a monarchical cast patriotism may look with indulgence, if not with favor, upon the spirit of party. But in those of the popular character, in governments purely elective, it is a spirit not to be encouraged. From their natural tendency it is certain there will always be enough of that spirit for every salutary purpose; and there being constant danger of excess, the effort ought to be by force of public opinion to mitigate and assuage it. A fire not to be quenched, it demands a uniform vigilance to prevent its bursting into a flame, lest, instead of warming, it should consume.

It is important, likewise, that the habits of thinking in a free country should inspire caution in those intrusted with its administration to confine themselves within their respective constitutional spheres, avoiding in the exercise of the powers of one department to encroach upon another. The spirit of encroachment tends to consolidate the powers of all the departments in one, and thus to create, whatever the form of government, a real despotism. A just estimate of that love of power and proneness to abuse it which predominates in the human heart is sufficient to satisfy us of the truth of this position. The necessity of reciprocal checks in the exercise of political power, by dividing and distributing it into different depositories, and constituting each the guardian of the public weal against invasions by the others, has been evinced by experiments ancient and modern, some of them in our country and under our own eyes. To preserve them must be as necessary as to institute them. If in the opinion of the people the distribution or modification of the constitutional powers be in any particular wrong, let it be corrected by an amendment in the way which the Constitution designates. But let there be no change by usurpation; for though this in one instance may be the instrument of good, it is the customary weapon by which free governments are destroyed. The precedent must always greatly overbalance in permanent evil any partial or transient benefit which the use can at any time yield.

Of all the dispositions and habits which lead to political prosperity, religion and morality are indispensable supports. In vain would that man claim the tribute of patriotism who should labor to subvert these great pillars of human happiness—these firmest props of the duties of men and citizens. The mere politician, equally with the pious man, ought to respect and to cherish them. A volume could not trace all their connections with private and public felicity. Let it simply be asked, Where is the security for property, for reputation, for life, if the sense of religious obligation desert the oaths which are the instruments of investigation in courts of justice? And let us with caution indulge the supposition that morality can be maintained without religion. Whatever may be conceded to the influence of refined education on minds of peculiar structure, reason and experience both forbid us to expect that national morality can prevail in exclusion of religious principle.

It is substantially true that virtue or morality is a necessary spring of popular government. The rule indeed extends with more or less force to every species of free government. Who that is a sincere friend to it can look with indifference upon attempts to shake the foundation of the fabric? Promote, then, as an object of primary importance, institutions for the general diffusion of knowledge. In proportion as the structure of a government gives force to public opinion, it is essential that public opinion should be enlightened.

As a very important source of strength and security, cherish public credit. One method of preserving it is to use it as sparingly as possible, avoiding occasions of expense by cultivating peace, but remembering also that timely disbursements to prepare for danger frequently prevent much greater disbursements to repel it; avoiding likewise the accumulation of debt, not only by shunning occasions of expense, but by vigorous exertions in time of peace to discharge the debts which unavoidable wars have occasioned, not ungenerously throwing upon posterity the burthen which we ourselves ought to bear. The execution of these maxims belongs to your representatives; but it is necessary that public opinion should cooperate. To facilitate to them the performance of their duty it is essential that you should practically bear in mind that toward the payment of debts there must be revenue; that to have revenue there must be taxes; that no taxes can be devised which are not more or less inconvenient and unpleasant; that the intrinsic embarrassment inseparable from the selection of the proper objects (which is always a choice of difficulties), ought to be a decisive motive for a candid construction of the conduct of the Government in making it, and for a spirit of acquiescence in the measures for obtaining revenue which the public exigencies may at any time dictate.

Observe good faith and justice toward all nations. Cultivate peace and harmony with all. Religion and morality enjoin this conduct. And can it be that good policy does not equally enjoin it? It will be worthy of a free, enlightened, and at no distant period a great nation to give to mankind the magnanimous and too novel example of a people always guided by an exalted justice and benevolence. Who can doubt that in the course of time and things the fruits of such a plan would richly repay any temporary advantages which might be lost by a steady adherence to it? Can it be that Providence has not connected the permanent felicity of a nation with its virtue? The experiment, at least, is recommended by every sentiment which ennobles human nature. Alas! is it rendered impossible by its vices?

In the execution of such a plan nothing is more essential than that permanent, inveterate antipathies against particular nations and passionate attachments for others should be excluded, and that in place of them just and amicable feelings toward all should be cultivated. The nation which indulges toward another an habitual hatred or an habitual fondness is in some degree a slave. It is a slave to its animosity or to its affection, either of which is sufficient to lead it astray from its duty and its interest. Antipathy in one nation against another disposes each more readily to offer insult and injury, to lay hold of slight causes of umbrage, and to be haughty and intractable when accidental or trifling occasions of dispute occur.

Hence frequent collisions, obstinate, envenomed, and bloody contests. The nation prompted by ill will and resentment sometimes impels to war the government contrary to the best calculations of policy. The government sometimes participates in the national propensity, and adopts through passion what reason would reject. At other times it makes the animosity of the nation subservient to projects of hostility, instigated by pride, ambition, and other sinister and pernicious motives. The peace often, sometimes perhaps the liberty, of nations has been the victim.

So, likewise, a passionate attachment of one nation for another produces a variety of evils. Sympathy for the favorite nation, facilitating the illusion of an imaginary common interest in cases where no real common interest exists, and infusing into one the enmities of the other, betrays the former into a participation in the quarrels and wars of the latter without adequate inducement or justification. It leads also to concessions to the favorite nation of privileges denied to others, which is apt doubly to injure the nation making the concessions by unnecessarily parting with what ought to have been retained, and by exciting jealousy, ill will, and a disposition to retaliate in the parties from whom equal privileges are withheld; and it gives to ambitious, corrupted, or deluded citizens (who devote themselves to the favorite nation) facility to betray or sacrifice the interests of their own country without odium, sometimes even with popularity, gilding with the appearances of a virtuous sense of obligation, a commendable deference for public opinion, or a laudable zeal for public good the base or foolish compliances of ambition, corruption, or infatuation.

As avenues to foreign influence in innumerable ways, such attachments are particularly alarming to the truly enlightened and independent patriot. How many opportunities do they afford to tamper with domestic factions, to practice the arts of seduction, to mislead public opinion, to influence or awe the public councils! Such an attachment of a small or weak toward a great and powerful nation dooms the former to be the satellite of the latter. Against the insidious wiles of foreign influence (I conjure you to believe me, fellow-citizens) the jealousy of a free people ought to be constantly awake, since history and experience prove that foreign influence is one of the most baneful foes of republican government. But that jealousy, to be useful, must be impartial, else it becomes the instrument of the very influence to be avoided, instead of a defense against it. Excessive partiality for one foreign nation and excessive dislike of another cause those whom they actuate to see danger only on one side, and serve to veil and even second the arts of influence on the other. Real patriots who may resist the intrigues of the favorite are liable to become suspected and odious, while its tools and dupes usurp the applause and confidence of the people to surrender their interests.

The great rule of conduct for us in regard to foreign nations is, in extending our commercial relations to have with them as little political connection as possible. So far as we have already formed engagements let them be fulfilled with perfect good faith. Here let us stop. Europe has a set of primary interests which to us have none or a very remote relation. Hence she must be engaged in frequent controversies, the causes of which are essentially foreign to our concerns. Hence, therefore, it must be unwise in us to implicate ourselves by artificial ties in the ordinary vicissitudes of her politics or the ordinary combinations and collisions of her friendships or enmities.

Our detached and distant situation invites and enables us to pursue a different course. If we remain one people, under an efficient government, the period is not far off when we may defy material injury from external annoyance; when we may take such an attitude as will cause the neutrality we may at any time resolve upon to be scrupulously respected; when belligerent nations, under the impossibility of making acquisitions upon us, will not lightly hazard the giving us provocation; when we may choose peace or war, as our interest, guided by justice, shall counsel.

Why forego the advantages of so peculiar a situation? Why quit our own to stand upon foreign ground? Why, by interweaving our destiny with that of any part of Europe, entangle our peace and prosperity in the toils of European ambition, rivalship, interest, humor, or caprice?

It is our true policy to steer clear of permanent alliances with any portion of the foreign world, so far, I mean, as we are now at liberty to do it; for let me not be understood as capable of patronizing infidelity to existing engagements. I hold the maxim no less applicable to public than to private affairs that honesty is always the best policy. I repeat, therefore, let those engagements be unwise to extend them.

Taking care always to keep ourselves by suitable establishments on a respectable defensive posture, we may safely trust to temporary alliances for extraordinary emergencies.

Harmony, liberal intercourse with all nations are recommended by policy, humanity, and interest. But even our commercial policy should hold an equal and impartial hand, neither seeking nor granting exclusive favors or preferences; consulting the natural course of things; diffusing and diversifying by gentle means the streams of commerce, but forcing nothing; establishing with powers so disposed, in order to give trade a stable course, to define the rights of our merchants, and to enable the Government to support them, conventional rules of intercourse, the best that present circumstances and mutual opinion will permit, but temporary and liable to be from time to time abandoned or varied as experience and circumstances shall dictate; constantly keeping in view that it is folly in one nation to look for disinterested favors from another; that it must pay with a portion of its independence for whatever it may accept under that character; that by such acceptance it may place itself in the condition of having given equivalents for nominal favors, and yet of being reproached with ingratitude for not giving more. There can be no greater error than to expect or calculate upon real favors from nation to nation. It is an illusion which experience must cure, which a just pride ought to discard.

In offering to you, my countrymen, these counsels of an old and affectionate friend I dare not hope they will make the strong and lasting impression I could wish—that they will control the usual current of the passions or prevent our nation from running the course which has hitherto marked the destiny of nations. But if I may even flatter myself that they may be productive of some partial benefit, some occasional good—that they may now and then recur to moderate the fury of party spirit, to warn against the mischiefs of foreign intrigue, to guard against the impostures of pretended patriotism—this hope will be a full recompense for the solicitude for your welfare by which they have been dictated.

How far in the discharge of my official duties I have been guided by the principles which have been delineated the public records and other evidences of my conduct must witness to you and to the world. To myself, the assurance of my own conscience is that I have at least believed myself to be guided by them.

In relation to the still subsisting war in Europe my proclamation of the 22d of April, 1793, is the index to my plan. Sanctioned by your approving voice and by that of your representatives in both Houses of Congress, the spirit of that measure has continually governed me, uninfluenced by any attempts to deter or divert me from it.

After deliberate examination, with the aid of the best lights I could obtain, I was well satisfied that our country, under all the circumstances of the case, had a right to take, and was bound in duty and interest to take, a neutral position. Having taken it, I determined as far as should depend upon me to maintain it with moderation, perseverance, and firmness.

The considerations which respect the right to hold this conduct it is not necessary on this occasion to detail. I will only observe that, according to my understanding of the matter, that right, so far from being denied by any of the belligerent powers, has been virtually admitted by all.

The duty of holding a neutral conduct may be inferred, without anything more, from the obligation which justice and humanity impose on every nation, in cases in which it is free to act, to maintain inviolate the relations of peace and amity toward other nations.

The inducements of interest for observing that conduct will best be referred to your own reflections and experience. With me a predominant motive has been to endeavor to gain time to our country to settle and mature its yet recent institutions, and to progress without interruption to that degree of strength and consistency which is necessary to give it, humanly speaking, the command of its own fortunes.

Though in reviewing the incidents of my Administration I am unconscious of intentional error, I am nevertheless too sensible of my defects not to think it probable that I may have committed many errors. Whatever they may be, I fervently beseech the Almighty to avert or mitigate the evils to which they may tend. I shall also carry with me the hope that my country will never cease to view them with indulgence, and that, after forty-five years of my life dedicated to its service with an upright zeal, the faults of incompetent abilities will be consigned to oblivion, as myself must soon be to the mansions of rest.

Relying on its kindness in this as in other things, and actuated by that fervent love toward it which is so natural to a man who views in it the native soil of himself and his progenitors for several generations, I anticipate with pleasing expectation that retreat in which I promise myself to realize without alloy the sweet enjoyment of partaking in the midst of my fellow-citizens the benign influence of good laws under a free government—the ever-favorite object of my heart, and the happy reward, as I trust, of our mutual cares, labors, and dangers.

ANDREW JACKSON

FAREWELL ADDRESS
SATURDAY, MARCH 4, 1837

March 4, 1837, was an important day in the history of the United States. As much as a day of new beginnings with the inauguration of a new president, Martin Van Buren, it was a day of farewell, as President Andrew Jackson, the last of the Revolutionary War heroes, the last president born as a British subject, was set to leave office. The ailing outgoing President Jackson and his vice president, Martin Van Buren, rode together to the Capitol from the White House in a carriage made of timbers from the U.S.S. Constitution. Well-wishers lined Pennsylvania Avenue. When the inaugural party reached the East Portico of the Capitol, Van Buren made his inaugural address and was sworn in to office. That same day, Jackson published his farewell address in the style of George Washington's. He addressed it to his "Fellow-Citizens" of the United States. On March 7, he left Washington and slowly returned to the Hermitage, his home in Tennessee, visiting his many friends in every town along the way.

Fellow-Citizens:

BEING ABOUT TO RETIRE finally from public life, I beg leave to offer you my grateful thanks for the many proofs of kindness and confidence which I have received at your hands. It has been my fortune in the discharge of public duties, civil and military, frequently to have found myself in difficult and trying situations, where prompt decision and energetic action were necessary, and where the interest of the country required that high responsibilities should be fearlessly encountered; and it is with the deepest emotions of gratitude that I acknowledge the continued and unbroken confidence with which you have sustained me in every trial. My public life has been a long one, and I can not hope that it has at all times been free from errors; but I have the consolation of knowing that if mistakes have been committed they have not seriously injured the country I so anxiously endeavored to serve, and at the moment when I surrender my last public trust I leave this great people prosperous and happy, in the full enjoyment of liberty and peace, and honored and respected by every nation of the world.

If my humble efforts have in any degree contributed to preserve to you these blessings, I have been more than rewarded by the honors you have heaped upon me, and, above all, by the generous confidence with which you have supported me in every peril, and with which you have continued to animate and cheer my path to the closing hour of my political life. The time has now come when advanced age and a broken frame warn me to retire from public concerns, but the recollection of the many favors you have bestowed upon me is engraven upon my heart, and I have felt that I could not part from your service without making this public acknowledgment of the gratitude I owe you. And if I use the occasion to offer to you the counsels of age and experience, you will, I trust, receive them with the same indulgent kindness which you have so often extended to me, and will at least see in them an earnest desire to perpetuate in this favored land the blessings of liberty and equal law.

We have now lived almost fifty years under the Constitution framed by the sages and patriots of the Revolution. The conflicts in which the nations of Europe were engaged during a great part of this period, the spirit in which they waged war against each other, and our intimate commercial connections with every part of the civilized world rendered it a time of much difficulty for the Government of the United States. We have had our seasons of peace and of war, with all the evils which precede or follow a state of hostility with powerful nations. We encountered these trials with our Constitution yet in its infancy, and under the disadvantages which a new and untried government must always feel when it is called upon to put forth its whole strength without the lights of experience to guide it or the weight of precedents to justify its measures. But we have passed triumphantly through all these difficulties. Our Constitution is no longer a doubtful experiment, and at the end of nearly half a century we find that it has preserved unimpaired the liberties of the people, secured the rights of property, and that our country has improved and is flourishing beyond any former example in the history of nations.

In our domestic concerns there is everything to encourage us, and if you are true to yourselves nothing can impede your march to the highest point of national prosperity. The States which had so long been retarded in their improvement by the Indian tribes residing in the midst of them are at length relieved from the evil, and this unhappy race—the original dwellers in our land—are now placed in a situation where we may well hope that they will share in the blessings of civilization and be saved from that degradation and destruction to which they were rapidly hastening while they remained in the States; and while the safety and comfort of our own citizens have been greatly promoted by their removal, the philanthropist will rejoice that the remnant of that ill-fated race has been at length placed beyond the reach of injury or oppression, and that the paternal care of the General Government will hereafter watch over them and protect them.

If we turn to our relations with foreign powers, we find our condition equally gratifying. Actuated by the sincere desire to do justice to every nation and to preserve the blessings of peace, our intercourse with them has been conducted on the part of this Government in the spirit of frankness; and I take pleasure in saying that it has generally been met in a corresponding temper. Difficulties of old standing have been surmounted by friendly discussion and the mutual desire to be just, and the claims of our citizens, which had been long withheld, have at length been acknowledged and adjusted and satisfactory arrangements made for their final payment; and with a limited, and I trust a temporary, exception, our relations with every foreign power are now of the most friendly character, our commerce continually expanding, and our flag respected in every quarter of the world.

These cheering and grateful prospects and these multiplied favors we owe, under Providence, to the adoption of the Federal Constitution. It is no longer a question whether this great country can remain happily united and flourish under our present form of government. Experience, the unerring test of all human undertakings, has shown the wisdom and foresight of those who formed it, and has proved that in the union of these States there is a sure foundation for the brightest hopes of freedom and for the happiness of the people. At every hazard and by every sacrifice this Union must be preserved.

The necessity of watching with jealous anxiety for the preservation of the Union was earnestly pressed upon his fellow-citizens by the Father of his Country in his Farewell Address. He has there told us that "while experience shall not have demonstrated its impracticability, there will always be reason to distrust the patriotism of those who in any quarter may endeavor to weaken its bands;" and he has cautioned us in the strongest terms against the formation of parties on geographical discriminations, as one of the means which might disturb our Union and to which designing men would be likely to resort.

The lessons contained in this invaluable legacy of Washington to his countrymen should be cherished in the heart of every citizen to the latest generation; and perhaps at no period of time could they be more usefully remembered than at the present moment; for when we look upon the scenes that are passing around us and dwell upon the pages of his parting address, his paternal counsels would seem to be not merely the offspring of wisdom and foresight, but the voice of prophecy, foretelling events and warning us of the evil to come. Forty years have passed since this imperishable document was given to his countrymen. The Federal Constitution was then regarded by him as an experiment—and he so speaks of it in his Address—but an experiment upon the success of which the best hopes of his country depended; and we all know that he was prepared to lay down his life, if necessary, to secure to it a full and a fair trial. The trial has been made. It has succeeded beyond the proudest hopes of those who framed it. Every quarter of this widely extended nation has felt its blessings and shared in the general prosperity produced by its adoption. But amid this general prosperity and splendid success the dangers of which he warned us are becoming every day more evident, and the signs of evil are sufficiently apparent to awaken the deepest anxiety in the bosom of the patriot. We behold systematic efforts publicly made to sow the seeds of discord between different parts of the United States and to place party divisions directly upon geographical distinctions; to excite the South against the North and the North against the South, and to force into the controversy the most delicate and exciting topics—topics upon which it is impossible that a large portion of the Union can ever speak without strong emotion. Appeals, too, are constantly made to sectional interests in order to influence the election of the Chief Magistrate, as if it were desired that he should favor a particular quarter of the country instead of fulfilling the duties of his station with impartial justice to all; and the possible dissolution of the Union has at length become an ordinary and familiar subject of discussion. Has the warning voice of Washington been forgotten, or have designs already been formed to sever the Union? Let it not be supposed that I impute to all of those who have taken an active part in these unwise and unprofitable discussions a want of patriotism or of public virtue. The honorable feeling of State pride and local attachments finds a place in the bosoms of the most enlightened and pure. But while such men are conscious of their own integrity and honesty of purpose, they ought never to forget that the citizens of other States are their political brethren, and that however mistaken they may be in their views, the great body of them are equally honest and upright with themselves. Mutual suspicions and reproaches may in time create mutual hostility, and artful and designing men will always be found who are ready to foment these fatal divisions and to inflame the natural jealousies of different sections of the country. The history of the world is full of such examples, and especially the history of republics.

What have you to gain by division and dissension? Delude not yourselves with the belief that a breach once made may be afterwards repaired. If the Union is once severed, the line of separation will grow wider and wider, and the controversies which are now debated and settled in the halls of legislation will then be tried in fields of battle and determined by the sword. Neither should you deceive yourselves with the hope that the first line of separation would be the permanent one, and that nothing but harmony and concord would be found in the new associations formed upon the dissolution of this Union. Local interests would still be found there, and unchastened ambition. And if the recollection of common dangers, in which the people of these United States stood side by side against the common foe, the memory of victories won by their united valor, the prosperity and happiness they have enjoyed under the present Constitution, the proud name they bear as citizens of this great Republic—if all these recollections and proofs of common interest are not strong enough to bind us together as one people, what tie will hold united the new divisions of empire when these bonds have been broken and this Union dissevered? The first line of separation would not last for a single generation; new fragments would be torn off, new leaders would spring up, and this great and glorious Republic would soon be broken into a multitude of petty States, without commerce, without credit, jealous of one another, armed for mutual aggression, loaded with taxes to pay armies and leaders, seeking aid against each other from foreign powers, insulted and trampled upon by the nations of Europe, until, harassed with conflicts and humbled and debased in spirit, they would be ready to submit to the absolute dominion of any military adventurer and to surrender their liberty for the sake of repose. It is impossible to look on the consequences that would inevitably follow the destruction of this Government and not feel indignant when we hear cold calculations about the value of the Union and have so constantly before us a line of conduct so well calculated to weaken its ties.

There is too much at stake to allow pride or passion to influence your decision. Never for a moment believe that the great body of the citizens of any State or States can deliberately intend to do wrong. They may, under the influence of temporary excitement or misguided opinions, commit mistakes; they may be misled for a time by the suggestions of self-interest; but in a community so enlightened and patriotic as the people of the United States argument will soon make them sensible of their errors, and when convinced they will be ready to repair them. If they have no higher or better motives to govern them, they will at least perceive that their own interest requires them to be just to others, as they hope to receive justice at their hands.

But in order to maintain the Union unimpaired it is absolutely necessary that the laws passed by the constituted authorities should be faithfully executed in every part of the country, and that every good citizen should at all times stand ready to put down, with the combined force of the nation, every attempt at unlawful resistance, under whatever pretext it may be made or whatever shape it may assume. Unconstitutional or oppressive laws may no doubt be passed by Congress, either from erroneous views or the want of due consideration; if they are within the reach of judicial authority, the remedy is easy and peaceful; and if, from the character of the law, it is an abuse of power not within the control of the judiciary, then free discussion and calm appeals to reason and to the justice of the people will not fail to redress the wrong. But until the law shall be declared void by the courts or repealed by Congress no individual or combination of individuals can be justified in forcibly resisting its execution. It is impossible that any government can continue to exist upon any other principles. It would cease to be a government and be unworthy of the name if it had not the power to enforce the execution of its own laws within its own sphere of action.

It is true that cases may be imagined disclosing such a settled purpose of usurpation and oppression on the part of the Government as would justify an appeal to arms. These, however, are extreme cases, which we have no reason to apprehend in a government where the power is in the hands of a patriotic people. And no citizen who loves his country would in any case whatever resort to forcible resistance unless he clearly saw that the time had come when a freeman should prefer death to submission; for if such a struggle is once begun, and the citizens of one section of the country arrayed in arms against those of another in doubtful conflict, let the battle result as it may, there will be an end of the Union and with it an end to the hopes of freedom. The victory of the injured would not secure to them the blessings of liberty; it would avenge their wrongs, but they would themselves share in the common ruin.

But the Constitution can not be maintained nor the Union preserved, in opposition to public feeling, by the mere exertion of the coercive powers confided to the General Government. The foundations must be laid in the affections of the people, in the security it gives to life, liberty, character, and property in every quarter of the country, and in the fraternal attachment which the citizens of the several States bear to one another as members of one political family, mutually contributing to promote the happiness of each other. Hence the citizens of every State should studiously avoid everything calculated to wound the sensibility or offend the just pride of the people of other States, and they should frown upon any proceedings within their own borders likely to disturb the tranquillity of their political brethren in other portions of the Union. In a country so extensive as the United States, and with pursuits so varied, the internal regulations of the several States must frequently differ from one another in important particulars, and this difference is unavoidably increased by the varying principles upon which the American colonies were originally planted—principles which had taken deep root in their social relations before the Revolution, and therefore of necessity influencing their policy since they became free and independent States. But each State has the unquestionable right to regulate its own internal concerns according to its own pleasure, and while it does not interfere with the rights of the people of other States or the rights of the Union, every State must be the sole judge of the measures proper to secure the safety of its citizens and promote their happiness; and all efforts on the part of people of other States to cast odium upon their institutions, and all measures calculated to disturb their rights of property or to put in jeopardy their peace and internal tranquillity, are in direct opposition to the spirit in which the Union was formed, and must endanger its safety. Motives of philanthropy may be assigned for this unwarrantable interference, and weak men may persuade themselves for a moment that they are laboring in the cause of humanity and asserting the rights of the human race; but everyone, upon sober reflection, will see that nothing but mischief can come from these improper assaults upon the feelings and rights of others. Rest assured that the men found busy in this work of discord are not worthy of your confidence, and deserve your strongest reprobation.

In the legislation of Congress also, and in every measure of the General Government, justice to every portion of the United States should be faithfully observed. No free government can stand without virtue in the people and a lofty spirit of patriotism, and if the sordid feelings of mere selfishness shall usurp the place which ought to be filled by public spirit, the legislation of Congress will soon be converted into a scramble for personal and sectional advantages. Under our free institutions the citizens of every quarter of our country are capable of attaining a high degree of prosperity and happiness without seeking to profit themselves at the expense of others; and every such attempt must in the end fail to succeed, for the people in every part of the United States are too enlightened not to understand their own rights and interests and to detect and defeat every effort to gain undue advantages over them; and when such designs are discovered it naturally provokes resentments which can not always be easily allayed. Justice—full and ample justice to every portion of the United States should be the ruling principle of every freeman, and should guide the deliberations of every public body, whether it be State or national.

It is well known that there have always been those amongst us who wish to enlarge the powers of the General Government, and experience would seem to indicate that there is a tendency on the part of this Government to overstep the boundaries marked out for it by the Constitution. Its legitimate authority is abundantly sufficient for all the purposes for which it was created, and its powers being expressly enumerated, there can be no justification for claiming anything beyond them. Every attempt to exercise power beyond these limits should be promptly and firmly opposed, for one evil example will lead to other measures still more mischievous; and if the principle of constructive powers or supposed advantages or temporary circumstances shall ever be permitted to justify the assumption of a power not given by the Constitution, the General Government will before long absorb all the powers of legislation, and you will have in effect but one consolidated government. From the extent of our country, its diversified interests, different pursuits, and different habits, it is too obvious for argument that a single consolidated government would be wholly inadequate to watch over and protect its interests; and every friend of our free institutions should be always prepared to maintain unimpaired and in full vigor the rights and sovereignty of the States and to confine the action of the General Government strictly to the sphere of its appropriate duties.

There is, perhaps, no one of the powers conferred on the Federal Government so liable to abuse as the taxing power. The most productive and convenient sources of revenue were necessarily given to it, that it might be able to perform the important duties imposed upon it; and the taxes which it lays upon commerce being concealed from the real payer in the price of the article, they do not so readily attract the attention of the people as smaller sums demanded from them directly by the taxgatherer. But the tax imposed on goods enhances by so much the price of the commodity to the consumer, and as many of these duties are imposed on articles of necessity which are daily used by the great body of the people, the money raised by these imposts is drawn from their pockets. Congress has no right under the Constitution to take money from the people unless it is required to execute some one of the specific powers intrusted to the Government; and if they raise more than is necessary for such purposes, it is an abuse of the power of taxation, and unjust and oppressive. It may indeed happen that the revenue will sometimes exceed the amount anticipated when the taxes were laid. When, however, this is ascertained, it is easy to reduce them, and in such a case it is unquestionably the duty of the Government to reduce them, for no circumstances can justify it in assuming a power not given to it by the Constitution nor in taking away the money of the people when it is not needed for the legitimate wants of the Government.

Plain as these principles appear to be, you will yet find there is a constant effort to induce the General Government to go beyond the limits of its taxing power and to impose unnecessary burdens upon the people. Many powerful interests are continually at work to procure heavy duties on commerce and to swell the revenue beyond the real necessities of the public service, and the country has already felt the injurious effects of their combined influence. They succeeded in obtaining a tariff of duties bearing most oppressively on the agricultural and laboring classes of society and producing a revenue that could not be usefully employed within the range of the powers conferred upon Congress, and in order to fasten upon the people this unjust and unequal system of taxation extravagant schemes of internal improvement were got up in various quarters to squander the money and to purchase support. Thus one unconstitutional measure was intended to be upheld by another, and the abuse of the power of taxation was to be maintained by usurping the power of expending the money in internal improvements. You can not have forgotten the severe and doubtful struggle through which we passed when the executive department of the Government by its veto endeavored to arrest this prodigal scheme of injustice and to bring back the legislation of Congress to the boundaries prescribed by the Constitution. The good sense and practical judgment of the people when the subject was brought before them sustained the course of the Executive, and this plan of unconstitutional expenditures for the purposes of corrupt influence is, I trust, finally overthrown.

The result of this decision has been felt in the rapid extinguishment of the public debt and the large accumulation of a surplus in the Treasury, notwithstanding the tariff was reduced and is now very far below the amount originally contemplated by its advocates. But, rely upon it, the design to collect an extravagant revenue and to burden you with taxes beyond the economical wants of the Government is not yet abandoned. The various interests which have combined together to impose a heavy tariff and to produce an overflowing Treasury are too strong and have too much at stake to surrender the contest. The corporations and wealthy individuals who are engaged in large manufacturing establishments desire a high tariff to increase their gains. Designing politicians will support it to conciliate their favor and to obtain the means of profuse expenditure for the purpose of purchasing influence in other quarters; and since the people have decided that the Federal Government can not be permitted to employ its income in internal improvements, efforts will be made to seduce and mislead the citizens of the several States by holding out to them the deceitful prospect of benefits to be derived from a surplus revenue collected by the General Government and annually divided among the States; and if, encouraged by these fallacious hopes, the States should disregard the principles of economy which ought to characterize every republican government, and should indulge in lavish expenditures exceeding their resources, they will before long find themselves oppressed with debts which they are unable to pay, and the temptation will become irresistible to support a high tariff in order to obtain a surplus for distribution. Do not allow yourselves, my fellow-citizens, to be misled on this subject. The Federal Government can not collect a surplus for such purposes without violating the principles of the Constitution and assuming powers which have not been granted. It is, moreover, a system of injustice, and if persisted in will inevitably lead to corruption, and must end in ruin. The surplus revenue will be drawn from the pockets of the people—from the farmer, the mechanic, and the laboring classes of society; but who will receive it when distributed among the States, where it is to be disposed of by leading State politicians, who have friends to favor and political partisans to gratify? It will certainly not be returned to those who paid it and who have most need of it and are honestly entitled to it. There is but one safe rule, and that is to confine the General Government rigidly within the sphere of its appropriate duties. It has no power to raise a revenue or impose taxes except for the purposes enumerated in the Constitution, and if its income is found to exceed these wants it should be forthwith reduced and the burden of the people so far lightened.

In reviewing the conflicts which have taken place between different interests in the United States and the policy pursued since the adoption of our present form of Government, we find nothing that has produced such deep-seated evil as the course of legislation in relation to the currency. The Constitution of the United States unquestionably intended to secure to the people a circulating medium of gold and silver. But the establishment of a national bank by Congress, with the privilege of issuing paper money receivable in the payment of the public dues, and the unfortunate course of legislation in the several States upon the same subject, drove from general circulation the constitutional currency and substituted one of paper in its place.

It was not easy for men engaged in the ordinary pursuits of business, whose attention had not been particularly drawn to the subject, to foresee all the consequences of a currency exclusively of paper, and we ought not on that account to be surprised at the facility with which laws were obtained to carry into effect the paper system. Honest and even enlightened men are sometimes misled by the specious and plausible statements of the designing. But experience has now proved the mischiefs and dangers of a paper currency, and it rests with you to determine whether the proper remedy shall be applied.

The paper system being founded on public confidence and having of itself no intrinsic value, it is liable to great and sudden fluctuations, thereby rendering property insecure and the wages of labor unsteady and uncertain. The corporations which create the paper money can not be relied upon to keep the circulating medium uniform in amount. In times of prosperity, when confidence is high, they are tempted by the prospect of gain or by the influence of those who hope to profit by it to extend their issues of paper beyond the bounds of discretion and the reasonable demands of business; and when these issues have been pushed on from day to day, until public confidence is at length shaken, then a reaction takes place, and they immediately withdraw the credits they have given, suddenly curtail their issues, and produce an unexpected and ruinous contraction of the circulating medium, which is felt by the whole community. The banks by this means save themselves, and the mischievous consequences of their imprudence or cupidity are visited upon the public. Nor does the evil stop here. These ebbs and flows in the currency and these indiscreet extensions of credit naturally engender a spirit of speculation injurious to the habits and character of the people. We have already seen its effects in the wild spirit of speculation in the public lands and various kinds of stock which within the last year or two seized upon such a multitude of our citizens and threatened to pervade all classes of society and to withdraw their attention from the sober pursuits of honest industry. It is not by encouraging this spirit that we shall best preserve public virtue and promote the true interests of our country; but if your currency continues as exclusively paper as it now is, it will foster this eager desire to amass wealth without labor; it will multiply the number of dependents on bank accommodations and bank favors; the temptation to obtain money at any sacrifice will become stronger and stronger, and inevitably lead to corruption, which will find its way into your public councils and destroy at no distant day the purity of your Government. Some of the evils which arise from this system of paper press with peculiar hardship upon the class of society least able to bear it. A portion of this currency frequently became depreciated or worthless, and all of it is easily counterfeited in such a manner as to require peculiar skill and much experience to distinguish the counterfeit from the genuine note. These frauds are most generally perpetrated in the smaller notes, which are used in the daily transactions of ordinary business, and the losses occasioned by them are commonly thrown upon the laboring classes of society, whose situation and pursuits put it out of their power to guard themselves from these impositions, and whose daily wages are necessary for their subsistence. It is the duty of every government so to regulate its currency as to protect this numerous class, as far as practicable, from the impositions of avarice and fraud. It is more especially the duty of the United States, where the Government is emphatically the Government of the people, and where this respectable portion of our citizens are so proudly distinguished from the laboring classes of all other nations by their independent spirit, their love of liberty, their intelligence, and their high tone of moral character. Their industry in peace is the source of our wealth and their bravery in war has covered us with glory; and the Government of the United States will but ill discharge its duties if it leaves them a prey to such dishonest impositions. Yet it is evident that their interests can not be effectually protected unless silver and gold are restored to circulation.

These views alone of the paper currency are sufficient to call for immediate reform; but there is another consideration which should still more strongly press it upon your attention.

Recent events have proved that the paper-money system of this country may be used as an engine to undermine your free institutions, and that those who desire to engross all power in the hands of the few and to govern by corruption or force are aware of its power and prepared to employ it. Your banks now furnish your only circulating medium, and money is plenty or scarce according to the quantity of notes issued by them. While they have capitals not greatly disproportioned to each other, they are competitors in business, and no one of them can exercise dominion over the rest; and although in the present state of the currency these banks may and do operate injuriously upon the habits of business, the pecuniary concerns, and the moral tone of society, yet, from their number and dispersed situation, they can not combine for the purposes of political influence, and whatever may be the dispositions of some of them their power of mischief must necessarily be confined to a narrow space and felt only in their immediate neighborhoods.

But when the charter for the Bank of the United States was obtained from Congress it perfected the schemes of the paper system and gave to its advocates the position they have struggled to obtain from the commencement of the Federal Government to the present hour. The immense capital and peculiar privileges bestowed upon it enabled it to exercise despotic sway over the other banks in every part of the country. From its superior strength it could seriously injure, if not destroy, the business of any one of them which might incur its resentment; and it openly claimed for itself the power of regulating the currency throughout the United States. In other words, it asserted (and it undoubtedly possessed) the power to make money plenty or scarce at its pleasure, at any time and in any quarter of the Union, by controlling the issues of other banks and permitting an expansion or compelling a general contraction of the circulating medium, according to its own will. The other banking institutions were sensible of its strength, and they soon generally became its obedient instruments, ready at all times to execute its mandates; and with the banks necessarily went also that numerous class of persons in our commercial cities who depend altogether on bank credits for their solvency and means of business, and who are therefore obliged, for their own safety, to propitiate the favor of the money power by distinguished zeal and devotion in its service. The result of the ill-advised legislation which established this great monopoly was to concentrate the whole moneyed power of the Union, with its boundless means of corruption and its numerous dependents, under the direction and command of one acknowledged head, thus organizing this particular interest as one body and securing to it unity and concert of action throughout the United States, and enabling it to bring forward upon any occasion its entire and undivided strength to support or defeat any measure of the Government. In the hands of this formidable power, thus perfectly organized, was also placed unlimited dominion over the amount of the circulating medium, giving it the power to regulate the value of property and the fruits of labor in every quarter of the Union, and to bestow prosperity or bring ruin upon any city or section of the country as might best comport with its own interest or policy.

We are not left to conjecture how the moneyed power, thus organized and with such a weapon in its hands, would be likely to use it. The distress and alarm which pervaded and agitated the whole country when the Bank of the United States waged war upon the people in order to compel them to submit to its demands can not yet be forgotten. The ruthless and unsparing temper with which whole cities and communities were oppressed, individuals impoverished and ruined, and a scene of cheerful prosperity suddenly changed into one of gloom and despondency ought to be indelibly impressed on the memory of the people of the United States. If such was its power in a time of peace, what would it not have been in a season of war, with an enemy at your doors? No nation but the freemen of the United States could have come out victorious from such a contest; yet, if you had not conquered, the Government would have passed from the hands of the many to the hands of the few, and this organized money power from its secret conclave would have dictated the choice of your highest officers and compelled you to make peace or war, as best suited their own wishes. The forms of your Government might for a time have remained, but its living spirit would have departed from it.

The distress and sufferings inflicted on the people by the bank are some of the fruits of that system of policy which is continually striving to enlarge the authority of the Federal Government beyond the limits fixed by the Constitution. The powers enumerated in that instrument do not confer on Congress the right to establish such a corporation as the Bank of the United States, and the evil consequences which followed may warn us of the danger of departing from the true rule of construction and of permitting temporary circumstances or the hope of better promoting the public welfare to influence in any degree our decisions upon the extent of the authority of the General Government. Let us abide by the Constitution as it is written, or amend it in the constitutional mode if it is found to be defective.

The severe lessons of experience will, I doubt not, be sufficient to prevent Congress from again chartering such a monopoly, even if the Constitution did not present an insuperable objection to it. But you must remember, my fellow-citizens, that eternal vigilance by the people is the price of liberty, and that you must pay the price if you wish to secure the blessing. It behooves you, therefore, to be watchful in your States as well as in the Federal Government. The power which the moneyed interest can exercise, when concentrated under a single head and with our present system of currency, was sufficiently demonstrated in the struggle made by the Bank of the United States. Defeated in the General Government, tho same class of intriguers and politicians will now resort to the States and endeavor to obtain there the same organization which they failed to perpetuate in the Union; and with specious and deceitful plans of public advantages and State interests and State pride they will endeavor to establish in the different States one moneyed institution with overgrown capital and exclusive privileges sufficient to enable it to control the operations of the other banks. Such an institution will be pregnant with the same evils produced by the Bank of the United States, although its sphere of action is more confined, and in the State in which it is chartered the money power will be able to embody its whole strength and to move together with undivided force to accomplish any object it may wish to attain. You have already had abundant evidence of its power to inflict injury upon the agricultural, mechanical, and laboring classes of society, and over those whose engagements in trade or speculation render them dependent on bank facilities the dominion of the State monopoly will be absolute and their obedience unlimited. With such a bank and a paper currency the money power would in a few years govern the State and control its measures, and if a sufficient number of States can be induced to create such establishments the time will soon come when it will again take the field against the United States and succeed in perfecting and perpetuating its organization by a charter from Congress.

It is one of the serious evils of our present system of banking that it enables one class of society—and that by no means a numerous one—by its control over the currency, to act injuriously upon the interests of all the others and to exercise more than its just proportion of influence in political affairs. The agricultural, the mechanical, and the laboring classes have little or no share in the direction of the great moneyed corporations, and from their habits and the nature of their pursuits they are incapable of forming extensive combinations to act together with united force. Such concert of action may sometimes be produced in a single city or in a small district of country by means of personal communications with each other, but they have no regular or active correspondence with those who are engaged in similar pursuits in distant places; they have but little patronage to give to the press, and exercise but a small share of influence over it; they have no crowd of dependents about them who hope to grow rich without labor by their countenance and favor, and who are therefore always ready to execute their wishes. The planter, the farmer, the mechanic, and the laborer all know that their success depends upon their own industry and economy, and that they must not expect to become suddenly rich by the fruits of their toil. Yet these classes of society form the great body of the people of the United States; they are the bone and sinew of the country— men who love liberty and desire nothing but equal rights and equal laws, and who, moreover, hold the great mass of our national wealth, although it is distributed in moderate amounts among the millions of freemen who possess it. But with overwhelming numbers and wealth on their side they are in constant danger of losing their fair influence in the Government, and with difficulty maintain their just rights against the incessant efforts daily made to encroach upon them. The mischief springs from the power which the moneyed interest derives from a paper currency which they are able to control, from the multitude of corporations with exclusive privileges which they have succeeded in obtaining in the different States, and which are employed altogether for their benefit; and unless you become more watchful in your States and check this spirit of monopoly and thirst for exclusive privileges you will in the end find that the most important powers of Government have been given or bartered away, and the control over your dearest interests has passed into the hands of these corporations.

The paper-money system and its natural associations—monopoly and exclusive privileges—have already struck their roots too deep in the soil, and it will require all your efforts to check its further growth and to eradicate the evil. The men who profit by the abuses and desire to perpetuate them will continue to besiege the halls of legislation in the General Government as well as in the States, and will seek by every artifice to mislead and deceive the public servants. It is to yourselves that you must look for safety and the means of guarding and perpetuating your free institutions. In your hands is rightfully placed the sovereignty of the country, and to you everyone placed in authority is ultimately responsible.

It is always in your power to see that the wishes of the people are carried into faithful execution, and their will, when once made known, must sooner or later be obeyed; and while the people remain, as I trust they ever will, uncorrupted and incorruptible, and continue watchful and jealous of their rights, the Government is safe, and the cause of freedom will continue to triumph over all its enemies.

But it will require steady and persevering exertions on your part to rid yourselves of the iniquities and mischiefs of the paper system and to check the spirit of monopoly and other abuses which have sprung up with it, and of which it is the main support. So many interests are united to resist all reform on this subject that you must not hope the conflict will be a short one nor success easy. My humble efforts have not been spared during my administration of the Government to restore the constitutional currency of gold and silver, and something, I trust, has been done toward the accomplishment of this most desirable object; but enough yet remains to require all your energy and perseverance. The power, however, is in your hands, and the remedy must and will be applied if you determine upon it.

While I am thus endeavoring to press upon your attention the principles which I deem of vital importance in the domestic concerns of the country, I ought not to pass over without notice the important considerations which should govern your policy toward foreign powers. It is unquestionably our true interest to cultivate the most friendly understanding with every nation and to avoid by every honorable means the calamities of war, and we shall best attain this object by frankness and sincerity in our foreign intercourse, by the prompt and faithful execution of treaties, and by justice and impartiality in our conduct to all. But no nation, however desirous of peace, can hope to escape occasional collisions with other powers, and the soundest dictates of policy require that we should place ourselves in a condition to assert our rights if a resort to force should ever become necessary. Our local situation, our long line of seacoast, indented by numerous bays, with deep rivers opening into the interior, as well as our extended and still increasing commerce, point to the Navy as our natural means of defense. It will in the end be found to be the cheapest and most effectual, and now is the time, in a season of peace and with an overflowing revenue, that we can year after year add to its strength without increasing the burdens of the people. It is your true policy, for your Navy will not only protect your rich and flourishing commerce in distant seas, but will enable you to reach and annoy the enemy and will give to defense its greatest efficiency by meeting danger at a distance from home. It is impossible by any line of fortifications to guard every point from attack against a hostile force advancing from the ocean and selecting its object, but they are indispensable to protect cities from bombardment, dockyards and naval arsenals from destruction, to give shelter to merchant vessels in time of war and to single ships or weaker squadrons when pressed by superior force. Fortifications of this description can not be too soon completed and armed and placed in a condition of the most perfect preparation. The abundant means we now possess can not be applied in any manner more useful to the country, and when this is done and our naval force sufficiently strengthened and our militia armed we need not fear that any nation will wantonly insult us or needlessly provoke hostilities. We shall more certainly preserve peace when it is well understood that we are prepared for War.

In presenting to you, my fellow-citizens, these parting counsels, I have brought before you the leading principles upon which I endeavored to administer the Government in the high office with which you twice honored me. Knowing that the path of freedom is continually beset by enemies who often assume the disguise of friends, I have devoted the last hours of my public life to warn you of the dangers. The progress of the United States under our free and happy institutions has surpassed the most sanguine hopes of the founders of the Republic. Our growth has been rapid beyond all former example in numbers, in wealth, in knowledge, and all the useful arts which contribute to the comforts and convenience of man, and from the earliest ages of history to the present day there never have been thirteen millions of people associated in one political body who enjoyed so much freedom and happiness as the people of these United States. You have no longer any cause to fear danger from abroad; your strength and power are well known throughout the civilized world, as well as the high and gallant bearing of your sons. It is from within, among yourselves—from cupidity, from corruption, from disappointed ambition and inordinate thirst for power—that factions will be formed and liberty endangered. It is against such designs, whatever disguise the actors may assume, that you have especially to guard yourselves. You have the highest of human trusts committed to your care. Providence has showered on this favored land blessings without number, and has chosen you as the guardians of freedom, to preserve it for the benefit of the human race. May He who holds in His hands the destinies of nations make you worthy of the favors He has bestowed and enable you, with pure hearts and pure hands and sleepless vigilance, to guard and defend to the end of time the great charge He has committed to your keeping.

My own race is nearly run; advanced age and failing health warn me that before long I must pass beyond the reach of human events and cease to feel the vicissitudes of human affairs. I thank God that my life has been spent in a land of liberty and that He has given me a heart to love my country with the affection of a son. And filled with gratitude for your constant and unwavering kindness, I bid you a last and affectionate farewell.

ANDREW JOHNSON

FAREWELL ADDRESS
THURSDAY, MARCH 4, 1869

In 1862, Senator Andrew Johnson of Tennessee first read George Washington's farewell address in front of the Senate. After the assassination of Abraham Lincoln in 1865, Andrew Johnson, then Lincoln's vice president, assumed the presidency. By 1868, under the shadow of Reconstruction, Andrew Johnson had become America's first impeached president. On March 4, 1869, President Johnson published his own farewell farewell address, using the opportunity to attack his enemies. He ended his address, "I have nothing to regret."

THE ROBE OF OFFICE by Constitutional limitation this day falls from my shoulders, to be immediately assumed by my successor. For him the forbearance and co-operation of the American people, in all his efforts to administer the Government within the pale of the Federal Constitution, are sincerely invoked. Without ambition to gratify, party ends to subserve, or personal quarrels to avenge, at the sacrifice of the peace and welfare of the country, my earnest desire is to see the Constitution of the Republic again recognized and obeyed as the supreme law of the land, and the whole people, North, South, East, and West, prosperous and happy under its wise provisions.

In surrendering the high office to which I was called four years ago, at a memorable and terrible crisis, it is my privilege, I trust, to say to the people of the United States a few parting words in vindication of an official course so ceaselessly assailed and aspersed by political leaders, to whose plans and wishes my policy to restore the Union has been obnoxious. In a period of difficulty and turmoil almost without precedent in the history of any people, consequent upon the closing scenes of a great rebellion and the assassination of the then President, it was perhaps too much on my part to expect of devoted partisans who rode on the waves of excitement, which at that time swept all before them, that degree of toleration and magnanimity which I sought to recommend and enforce and which I believe in good time would have advanced us infinitely further on the road to permanent peace and prosperity than we have thus far attained. Doubtless had I, at the commencement of my term of office, unhesitatingly lent its powers, or perverted them to purposes and plans outside of the Constitution, and become an instrument to schemes of confiscation and of general and oppressive disqualification, I would have been hailed as all that was true, loyal, and discerning, as the reliable head of a party, whatever I might have been as the Executive of a Nation. Unwilling, however, to accede to propositions of extremists, and bound to obey at every personal hazard my oath to defend the Constitution, I need not perhaps be surprised at having met the fate of others whose only rewards for upholding Constitutional rights and laws have been the consciousness of having attempted to do their duty, and the calm judgment of history. At the time a mysterious Providence assigned to me the office of President, I was, by the terms of the Constitution, the Commander-in-Chief of nearly a million of men under arms. One of my first acts was to disband and restore to the vocations of civil life this immense host, and to divest myself so far as I could of the unparalleled powers then incident to the office and the times. Whether or not in this step I was right, and how far deserving of the approbation of all the people, all can now on reflection judge, when reminded of the ruinous condition of public affairs that must have resulted from the continuance in the military service of such a vast number of men. The close of our domestic conflict found the army eager to distinguish itself in a new field by an effort to punish European intervention in Mexico. By many it was believed and urged that, aside from the assumed justice of the proceeding, a foreign war in which both sides would cheerfully unite to vindicate the honor of the national flag and further illustrate the national prowess, would be the surest and speediest way of awakening national enthusiasm, reviving devotion to the Union, and occupying a force concerning which grave doubts existed as to its willingness, after four years of active campaigning, at once to return to the pursuits of peace: Whether these speculations were true or false, it will be conceded that they existed, and that the predilections of the army were for the time being in the direction indicated. Taking advantage of that feeling it would have been easy as the Commander-in-Chief of the army and navy, and with all the power and patronage of the Presidential office at my disposal, to turn the concentrated strength of the Nation against French interference in Mexico, and to inaugurate a movement which would have been received with favor by the military and a large portion of the people. It is proper in this connection that I should refer to the almost unlimited additional powers tendered to the Executive by the measures relating to Civil Rights and the Freedmen's Bureau, contrary to most precedents in the experience of public men. The powers thus placed within my grasp were declined as being in violation of the Constitution, dangerous to the liberties of the people, and tending to aggravate rather than lessen the discords naturally resulting from our Civil War. With a large army and augmented authority, it would have been no difficult task to direct at pleasure the destinies of the Republic, and to make secure my continuance in the highest office known to our laws. Let the people, whom I am addressing from the Presidential Chair during the closing hours of a laborious term, consider how different would have been their present condition had I yielded to the dazzling temptation of foreign conquest, of personal aggrandizement, and the desire to wield additional power. Let them with justice consider that I have not unduly magnified mine office, the public burdens have not been increased by my acts, and perhaps thousands or tens of thousands of lives sacrificed to visions of false glory. It can not, therefore, be charged that my ambition has been of that ordinary or criminal kind which, to the detriment of the people's rights and liberties, ever seeks to grasp more and unwarranted powers, and to accomplish its purposes panders too often to popular prejudice and party aims.

What, then, have been the aspirations which guided me in my official acts? Those acts need not at this time an elaborate explanation. They have elsewhere been comprehensively stated and fully discussed, and become a part of the nation's history. By them I am ready to be judged, knowing that, however imperfect, they at least show to the impartial mind that my sole ambition has been to restore the Union of the States, faithfully to execute the office of President, and to the best of my ability to preserve, protect, and defend the Constitution. I can not be censured if my efforts have been impeded in the interests of party faction, and if a policy, which was intended to reassure and conciliate the people of both sections of the country, was made the occasion of inflaming and dividing still further those who, only recently in arms against each other, yet as individuals and citizens were sincerely desirous, as I shall ever believe, of burying all hostile feelings in the grave of the past. The bitter war was waged on the part of the Government to vindicate the Constitution, and save the Union; and if I have erred in trying to bring about a more speedy and lasting peace, to extinguish heart-burnings and enmities, and to prevent trouble in the South, which, retarding material prosperity in that region, injuriously affected the whole country, I am quite content to rest my case with the more deliberate judgment of the people, and, as I have already intimated, with the distant future. The war, all must remember, was a stupendous and deplorable mistake. Neither side understood the other, and had this simple fact and its conclusions been kept in view, all that was needed was accomplished by the acknowledgment of the terrible wrong, and the expression of better feeling, and earnest endeavor at atonement shown and felt. In the prompt ratification of Constitutional amendments by the Southern States at the close of the war, not accepting the war as a confessed false step on the part of those who inaugurated it, was an error which now only time can cure, and which, even at this late date, we should endeavor to palliate, experiencing, moreover, as all have done, the frightful cost of the arbitrament of the sword. Let us in the future, cling closer than ever to the Constitution as our only safeguard. It is to be hoped that not until the burdens now pressing upon us with such fearful weight are removed, will our people forget the lessons of the war, and that, remembering them from whatever cause, peace between sections and States may be perpetual.

The history of late events in our country, as well as of the greatest governments of ancient and modern times, teaches that we have every thing to fear from a departure from the letter and spirit of the Constitution, and the undue ascendency of men allowed to assume power in what are considered desperate emergencies. Sylla, on becoming master of Rome, at once adopted measures to crush his enemies and to consolidate the power of his party. He established military colonies throughout Italy, deprived of the full Roman franchise the inhabitants of the Italian towns who had opposed his usurpation, confiscated their lands and gave them to his soldiers, and conferred citizenship upon a great number of slaves belonging to those who had proscribed him, thus creating at Rome a kind of bodyguard for his protection. After having given Rome over to slaughter, and tyrannized beyond all example over those opposed to him and the legions, his terrible instrument of wrong, Sylla could yet feel safe in laying down the ensigns of power so dreadfully abused, and in mingling freely with the families and friends of his myriad victims. The fear which he had inspired continued after his voluntary abdication, and even in retirement his will was law to a people who had permitted themselves to be enslaved. What but a subtle knowledge and conviction that the Roman people had become changed, discouraged, and utterly broken in spirit could have induced this daring assumption? What but public indifference to consequences so terrible as to leave Rome open to every calamity, which subsequently befell her, could have justified the conclusions of the dictator and tyrant in his startling experiment?

We find that in the time which has since elapsed human nature and exigencies in governments have not greatly changed. Who, a few years ago, in contemplating our future, could have supposed that in a brief period of bitter experience, every thing demanded in the name of military emergency or dictated by caprice would come to be considered as mere matters of course; that conscription, confiscation, loss of personal liberty, the subjection of States to military rule and disfranchisement, with the extension of the right of suffrage merely to accomplish party ends, would receive the passive submission, if not acquiescence, of the people of the Republic? It has been clearly demonstrated by recent occurrences that encroachments upon the Constitution can not be prevented by the

President, however devoted or determined he may be; that unless the people interpose there is no power under the Constitution to check a dominant majority of two-thirds of the Congress of the United States. An appeal to the nation is attended with too much delay to meet emergency; while if left free to act, the people would correct in time such evils as might follow legislative usurpation. There is danger that the same power which disregards the Constitution will deprive them of the right to change their rulers except by revolution. We have already seen the jurisdiction of the judiciary circumscribed when it was apprehended that the courts would decide against laws having for their sole object the supremacy of party, while the veto power lodged in the Executive by the Constitution for the interest and protection of the people, and exercised by Washington and his successors, has been rendered nugatory by a partisan majority of two-thirds in each branch of the National Legislature. The Constitution evidently contemplates that when a bill is returned with the President's objections, it will be calmly reconsidered by Congress. Such, however, has not been the practice under the present party rule. It has become evident that men who pass a bill under partisan influences are not likely, through patriotic motives, to admit their error, and thereby weaken their own organizations by solemnly confessing it under the official oath. Pride of opinion, if nothing else, has intervened and prevented a calm and dispassionate reconsideration of a bill disapproved by the Executive.

Much as I venerate the Constitution, it must be admitted that this condition of affairs has developed a defect which, the aggressive tendency of the Legislative Department of the Government, may readily work its overthrow. It may, however, be remedied without disturbing the harmony of the instrument. The veto power is generally exercised upon Constitutional grounds, and whenever it is so applied, and the bill returned with the Executive's reasons for withholding his signature, it ought to be immediately certified to the Supreme Court of the United States for its decision. If its Constitutionality shall be declared by that tribunal, it should then become a law. But if the decision is otherwise, it should fail without power in Congress to re-enact and make it valid. In cases in which the veto rests upon hasty and inconsiderate legislation, and in which no Constitutional question is involved, I would not change the fundamental law; for, in such cases no permanent evil can be incorporated into the Federal system. It is obvious that without such an amendment the Government, as it existed under the Constitution prior to the Rebellion, may be wholly subverted and overthrown by a two-thirds majority in Congress. It is not, therefore, difficult to see how easily and how rapidly the people, may lose (shall I not say have lost?) their liberties by an unchecked and uncontrollable majority in the law-making power; and, whenever deprived of their rights, how powerless they are to regain them?

Let us turn for a moment to the history of the majority in Congress, which has acted in such utter disregard of the Constitution, while public attention has been carefully and constantly turned to the past and expiated sins of the South, and the servants of the people in high places have boldly betrayed their trust, broken their oaths of obedience to the Constitution, and undermined the very foundations of liberty, justice, and good government. When the Rebellion was being suppressed by the volunteered services of patriot soldiers, amid the dangers of the battle-field, these men crept, without question, into place and power in the national councils. After all dangers had passed, when no armed foe remained—when a penitent people bowed their heads to the flag and renewed their allegiance to the Government of the United States, then it was that pretended patriots appeared before the Nation and began to prate about the thousands of lives and millions of treasure sacrificed in the suppression of the Rebellion. They have since persistently sought to inflame the prejudices engendered between the sections, to retard the restoration of peace and harmony, and by every means to keep open and exposed to the poisonous breath of party passion the terrible wounds of a four years' war. They have prevented the return of peace, and the restoration of the Union; in every way rendered delusive the purposes, promises, and pledges by which the army was marshaled, treason rebuked, and rebellion crushed; and made the liberties of the people, and the rights and powers of the President, objects of constant attack. They have wrested from the President his Constitutional power of supreme command of the army and navy; they have destroyed the strength and efficiency of the Executive Department by making subordinate officers independent of, and able to defy, their chief; they have attempted to place the President under the power of a bold, defiant, and treacherous cabinet officer; they have robbed the Executive of the prerogative of pardon, rendered null and void acts of clemency granted to thousands of persons under the provisions of the Constitution, and committed gross usurpation by legislative attempts to exercise this power in favor of party adherents; they have conspired to change the system of our Government by preferring charges against the President in the form of articles of impeachment, and contemplating before hearing or trial that he should be placed in arrest, held in durance, and when it became their pleasure to pronounce his sentence, driven from place and power in disgrace; they have in time of peace increased the national debt by a reckless expenditure of the public moneys, and thus added to the burdens which already weigh upon the people; they have permitted the nation to suffer the evils of a deranged currency to the enhancement in price of all the necessaries of life; they have maintained a large standing army for the enforcement of their measures of oppression; they have engaged in class legislation, and built up and encouraged monopolies that the few might be enriched at the expense of the many; they have failed to act upon important treaties, thereby endangering our present peaceful relations with foreign powers. Their course of usurpation has not been limited to inroads upon the Executive Department. By unconstitutional and oppressive enactments the people of ten States of the Union have been reduced to a condition more intolerable than that from which the patriots of the Revolution rebelled. Millions of American citizens can now say of their oppressors, with more truth than our fathers did of British tyrants, that they have "forbidden the Governments to pass laws of immediate and pressing importance, unless suspended until their assent should be obtained;" that they have "refused to pass other laws for the accommodation of large districts of people, unless those people would relinquish the right of representation in the Legislature, a right inestimable to them and formidable to tyrants only;" that they have "made judges dependent upon their will alone for the tenure of their offices and the amount and payment of their salaries;" that they have erected a multitude of new offices and sent further swarms of officers to harass our people and eat out their substance; that they have affected to render the military independent and superior to the civil power; combined with others to subject us to a jurisdiction foreign to our Constitution and unacknowledged by our laws; quartered large bodies of armed troops among us; protected them by a mock trial from punishment for any murders which they should commit on the inhabitants of these States; imposed taxes upon us without our consent; deprived us in many cases of the benefit of trial by jury; taken away our charters; incited domestic insurrection among us; abolished our most valuable laws; altered fundamentally the forms of our Government; suspended our own Legislatures, and declared themselves invested with power to legislate for us in all cases whatsoever.

This catalogue of crimes, long as it is, is not yet complete. The Constitution vests the judicial power of the United States in one Supreme Court, whose jurisdiction shall extend to all cases arising under the Constitution and the laws of the United States. Encouraged by this promise of a refuge from tyranny, a citizen of the United States, who by the order of a military commander, given under the sanction of a cruel and deliberate edict of Congress, had been denied the Constitutional rights of liberty of conscience, freedom of the press and of speech, personal freedom from military arrest, of being held to answer for crime only upon presentment of an indictment, of trial by jury, of the writ of habeas corpus and the protection of a civil and Constitutional Government—a citizen thus deeply wronged appeals to the Supreme Court for the protection guaranteed him by the organic law of the land. At once a fierce and excited majority, by the ruthless hand of legislative power, stripped the ermine from the Judges, transferred the sword of justice to the General, and remanded the oppressed citizen to a degradation and bondage worse than death. It will also be recorded as one of the marvels of the times that a party claiming for itself a monopoly of consistency and patriotism, and boasting of its unlimited sway, endeavored, by a costly and deliberate trial, to impeach one who defended the Constitution and the Union, not only throughout the War of the Rebellion, but during the whole term of office as Chief Magistrate, but, at the same time, could find no warrant or means at their command to bring to trial even the chief of the Rebellion. Indeed, the remarkable failures in this case were so often repeated that, for propriety's sake, if for no other reason, it became at last necessary to extend to him an unconditional pardon. What more plainly than this illustrates the extremity of party management and inconsistency on one hand, and of faction, vindictiveness, and intolerance on the other? Patriotism will hardly be encouraged when, in such a record, it sees that its instant reward may be most virulent party abuse and obloquy, if not attempted disgrace. Instead of seeking to make treason odious, it would, in truth, seem to have been their purpose rather to make the defense of the Constitution and Union a crime, and to punish fidelity to an oath of office, if counter to party dictation, by all the means at their command.

Happily for the peace of the country, the war has determined against the assumed power of the States to withdraw at pleasure from the Union. The institution of slavery, also, found its destruction in a Rebellion commenced in its interest. It should be borne in mind, however, that the war neither impaired nor destroyed the Constitution, but on the contrary, preserved its existence, and made apparent its real power and enduring strength. All the rights granted to the States or reserved to the people are therefore intact. Among those rights is that of the people of each State to declare the qualifications of their own State electors. It is now assumed that Congress can control this vital right, which can never be taken away from the States without impairing the fundamental principle of the Government itself. It is necessary to the existence of the States as well as to the protection of the liberties of the people; for the right to select the elector in whom the political power of the State shall be lodged, involves the right of the State to govern itself. When deprived of this prerogative, the State will have no power worth retaining. All will be gone, and they will be subjected to the arbitrary will of Congress. The Government will then be centralized, if not by the passage of laws, then by the adoption, through partisan influence, of an amendment directly in conflict with the original design of the Constitution. This proves how necessary it is the people should require the administration of the three great departments of the Government to be strictly within the limits of the Constitution. Their boundaries have been accurately defined, and neither should be allowed to trespass on the other; nor, above all, to encroach upon the reserved rights of the people and the States. The troubles of the past four years will prove to the Nation blessings, if they produce so desirable a result.

Upon those who become young men amid the sound of cannon and the din of arms, and who quietly returned to the farms, the factories, and the schools of the land, will principally devolve the solemn duty of perpetuating the Union of the States, in defense of which hundreds of thousands of their comrades expired, and hundreds of millions of national obligations were incurred. A manly people will not neglect the training necessary to resist aggression, but they should be jealous lest the civil be made subordinate to the military element. We need to encourage in every legitimate way a study of the Constitution for which the war was waged; a knowledge of, and reverence for, whose wise checks, by those so soon to occupy the places filled by their seniors, will be the only hope of preserving the Republic. The young men of the Nation, not yet under the control of party, must resist the tendency to centralization, an outgrowth of the great Rebellion, and be familiar with the fact that the country consists of the "United States," and that where the States surrendered certain great rights for the sake of a more perfect Union, they retained rights as valuable and important as those they relinquished for the common weal. This sound old doctrine, far different from the teachings that led to the attempt to secede, and a kindred theory, that the States were taken out of the Union by the rash acts of conspirators that happened to dwell within their borders, must be received and advocated with the enthusiasm of early manhood, or the people will be ruled by corrupt combinations of the commercial centers, which, plethoric from wealth, annually migrate to the Capital of the Nation to purchase special legislation. Until the Representatives of the people in Congress more fully exhibit the diverse views, and the interests of the whole Nation and laws cease to be made without full discussion at the behest of some party leader, there will never be a proper respect shown by the law-making power either to the Judicial or Executive branch of the Government. The generation just beginning to use the ballot-box, it is believed, only need that their attention should be called to these considerations to indicate by their votes that they wish their Representatives to observe all the restraints which the people, in adopting the Constitution, intended to impose on party excess.

Calmly reviewing my administration of the Government, I feel that (with a sense of accountability to God, having conscientiously endeavored to discharge my whole duty) I have nothing to regret. Events have proved the correctness of the policy set forth in my first and subsequent messages. The woes which have followed the rejection of forbearance, magnanimity, and Constitutional rule are known and deplored by the Nation. It is a matter of pride and gratification, in retiring from the most exalted position in the gift of a free people, to feel and know that in a long, arduous and eventful public life my action has never been influenced by desire for gain, and that I can in all sincerity inquire. Whom have I defrauded? Whom have I oppressed? or, At whose hand have I received any bribe to blind ray eyes therewith? No responsibility for wars that have been waged or blood that has been shed rests upon me. My thoughts have been those of peace, and my effort has ever been to allay contentions among my countrymen. Forgetting the past, let us return to the first principles of the Government, and unfurling the banner of our country, inscribe upon it in ineffaceable characters, "The Constitution and the Union, one and inseparable."

HARRY S. TRUMAN

FAREWELL ADDRESS
FRIDAY, JANUARY 15, 1953

On January 15, 1953, Harry S. Truman made the first farewell address by an American president in more than eighty years. It was also the first farewell speech, as the first three addresses had all appeared in print. President Truman made this speech from the Oval Office directly to the American people via radio and television.

My fellow Americans:

I AM HAPPY to have this opportunity to talk to you once more before I leave the White House.

Next Tuesday, General Eisenhower will be inaugurated as President of the United States. A short time after the new President takes his oath of office, I will be on the train going back home to Independence, Missouri. I will once again be a plain, private citizen of this great Republic.

That is as it should be. Inauguration Day will be a great demonstration of our democratic process. I am glad to be a part of it—glad to wish General Eisenhower all possible success, as he begins his term—glad the whole world will have a chance to see how simply and how peacefully our American system transfers the vast power of the Presidency from my hands to his. It is a good object lesson in democracy. I am very proud of it. And I know you are, too.

During the last 2 months I have done my best to make this transfer an orderly one. I have talked with my successor on the affairs of the country, both foreign and domestic, and my Cabinet officers have talked with their successors. I want to say that General Eisenhower and his associates have cooperated fully in this effort. Such an orderly transfer from one party to another has never taken place before in our history. I think a real precedent has been set.

In speaking to you tonight, I have no new revelations to make—no political statements—no policy announcements. There are simply a few things in my heart that I want to say to you. I want to say "goodbye" and "thanks for your help." And I want to talk to you a little while about what has happened since I became your President.

I am speaking to you from the room where I have worked since April 12, 1945. This is the President's office in the West Wing of the

White House. This is the desk where I have signed most of the papers that embodied the decisions I have made as President. It has been the desk of many Presidents, and will be the desk of many more.

Since I became President, I have been to Europe, Mexico, Canada, Brazil, Puerto Rico, and the Virgin Islands—Wake Island and Hawaii. I have visited almost every State in the Union. I have traveled 135,000 miles by air, 77,000 by rail, and 17,000 by ship. But the mail always followed me, and wherever I happened to be, that's where the office of the President was.

The greatest part of the President's job is to make decisions—big ones and small ones, dozens of them almost every day. The papers may circulate around the Government for a while but they finally reach this desk. And then, there's no place else for them to go. The President— whoever he is—has to decide. He can't pass the buck to anybody. No one else can do the deciding for him. That's his job.

That's what I've been doing here in this room, for almost 8 years. And over in the main part of the White House, there's a study on the second floor—a room much like this one—where I have worked at night and early in the morning on the papers I couldn't get to at the office.

Of course, for more than 3 years Mrs. Truman and I were not living in the White House. We were across the street in the Blair House. That was when the White House almost fell down on us and had to be rebuilt. I had a study over at the Blair House, too, but living in the Blair House was not as convenient as living in the White House. The Secret Service wouldn't let me walk across the street, so I had to get in a car every morning to cross the street to the White House office, again at noon to go to the Blair House for lunch, again to go back to the office after lunch, and finally take an automobile at night to return to the Blair House. Fantastic, isn't it? But necessary, so my guards thought—and they are the bosses on such matters as that.

Now, of course, we're back in the White House. It is in very good condition, and General Eisenhower will be able to take up his residence in the house and work right here. That will be much more convenient for him, and I'm very glad the renovation job was all completed before his term began.

Your new President is taking office in quite different circumstances than when I became President 8 years ago. On April 1945, I had been presiding over the Senate in my capacity as Vice President. When the Senate recessed about 5 o'clock in the afternoon, I walked over to the office of the Speaker of the House, Mr. Rayburn, to discuss pending legislation. As soon as I arrived, I was told that Mr. Early, one of President

Roosevelt's secretaries, wanted me to call. I reached Mr. Early, and he told me to come to the White House as quickly as possible, to enter by way of the Pennsylvania Avenue entrance, and to come to Mrs. Roosevelt's study.

When I arrived, Mrs. Roosevelt told me the tragic news, and I felt the shock that all of you felt a little later—when the word came over the radio and appeared in the newspapers. President Roosevelt had died. I offered to do anything I could for Mrs. Roosevelt, and then I asked the Secretary of State to call the Cabinet together.

At 7:09 P.M. I was sworn in as President by Chief Justice Stone in the Cabinet Room.

Things were happening fast in those days. The San Francisco conference to organize the United Nations had been called for April 25th. I was asked if that meeting would go forward. I announced that it would. That was my first decision.

After attending President Roosevelt's funeral, I went to the Hall of the House of Representatives and told a joint session of the Congress that I would carry on President Roosevelt's policies.

On May 7th, Germany surrendered. The announcement was made on May 8th, my 61st birthday.

Mr. Churchill called me shortly after that and wanted a meeting with me and Prime Minister Stalin of Russia. Later on, a meeting was agreed upon, and Churchill, Stalin, and I met at Potsdam in Germany.

Meanwhile, the first atomic explosion took place out in the New Mexico desert.

The war against Japan was still going on. I made the decision that the atomic bomb had to be used to end it. I made that decision in the conviction it would save hundreds of thousands of lives—Japanese as well as American. Japan surrendered, and we were faced with the huge problems of bringing the troops home and reconverting the economy from war to peace.

All these things happened within just a little over 4 months—from April to August 1945. I tell you this to illustrate the tremendous scope of the work your President has to do.

And all these emergencies and all the developments to meet them have required the President to put in long hours—usually 17 hours a day, with no payment for overtime. I sign my name, on the average, 600 times a day, see and talk to hundreds of people every month, shake hands with thousands every year, and still carry on the business of the largest going concern in the whole world. There is no job like it on the face of the earth—in the power which is concentrated here at this desk, and in the responsibility and difficulty of the decisions.

I want all of you to realize how big a job, how hard a job, it is—not for my sake, because I am stepping out of it—but for the sake of my successor. He needs the understanding and the help of every citizen. It is not enough for you to come out once every 4 years and vote for a candidate, and then go back home and say, "Well, I've done my part, now let the new President do the worrying." He can't do the job alone.

Regardless of your politics, whether you are Republican or Democrat, your fate is tied up with what is done here in this room. The President is President of the whole country. We must give him our support as citizens of the United States. He will have mine, and I want you to give him yours.

I suppose that history will remember my term in office as the years when the "cold war" began to overshadow our lives. I have had hardly a day in office that has not been dominated by this all—embracing struggle—this conflict between those who love freedom and those who would lead the world back into slavery and darkness. And always in the background there has been the atomic bomb.

But when history says that my term of office saw the beginning of the cold war, it will also say that in those 8 years we have set the course that can win it. We have succeeded in carving out a new set of policies to attain peace—positive policies, policies of world leadership, policies that express faith in other free people. We have averted world war III up to now, and we may already have succeeded in establishing conditions which can keep that war from happening as far ahead as man can see.

These are great and historic achievements that we can all be proud of. Think of the difference between our course now and our course 30 years ago. After the First World War we withdrew from world affairs—we failed to act in concert with other peoples against aggression—we helped to kill the League of Nations—and we built up tariff barriers that strangled world trade. This time, we avoided those mistakes. We helped to found and sustain the United Nations. We have welded alliances that include the greater part of the free world. And we have gone ahead with other free countries to help build their economies and link us all together in a healthy world trade.

Think back for a moment to the 1930's and you will see the difference. The Japanese moved into Manchuria, and free men did not act. The Fascists moved into Ethiopia, and we did not act. The Nazis marched into the Rhineland, into Austria, into Czechoslovakia, and free men were paralyzed for lack of strength and unity and will.

Think about those years of weakness and indecision, and the World War II which was their evil result. Then think about the speed and courage and decisiveness with which we have moved against the Communist threat since World War II.

The first crisis came in 1945 and 1946, when the Soviet Union refused to honor its agreement to remove its troops from Iran. Members of my Cabinet came to me and asked if we were ready to take the risk that a firm stand involved. I replied that we were. So we took our stand—we made it clear to the Soviet Union that we expected them to honor their agreement—and the Soviet troops were withdrawn from Iran.

Then, in early 1947, the Soviet Union threatened Greece and Turkey. The British sent me a message saying they could no longer keep their forces in that area. Something had to be done at once, or the eastern Mediterranean would be taken over by the Communists. On March 12th, I went before the Congress and stated our determination to help the people of Greece and Turkey maintain their independence. Today, Greece is still free and independent; and Turkey is a bulwark of strength at a strategic corner of the world.

Then came the Marshall plan which saved Europe, the heroic Berlin airlift, and our military aid programs.

We inaugurated the North Atlantic Pact, the Rio Pact binding the Western Hemisphere together, and the defense pacts with countries of the Far Pacific.

Most important of all, we acted in Korea. I was in Independence, Missouri, in June 1950, when Secretary Acheson telephoned me and gave me the news about the invasion of Korea. I told the Secretary to lay the matter at once before the United Nations, and I came on back to Washington.

Flying back over the flatlands of the Middle West and over the Appalachians that summer afternoon, I had a lot of time to think. I turned the problem over in my mind in many ways, but my thoughts kept coming back to the 1930's—to Manchuria, to Ethiopia, the Rhineland, Austria, and finally to Munich.

Here was history repeating itself. Here was another probing action, another testing action. If we let the Republic of Korea go under, some other country would be next, and then another. And all the time, the courage and confidence of the free world would be ebbing away, just as it did in the 1930's. And the United Nations would go the way of the League of Nations.

When I reached Washington, I met immediately with the Secretary of State, the Secretary of Defense, and General Bradley, and the other civilian and military officials who had information and advice to help me decide on what to do. We talked about the problems long and hard. We considered those problems very carefully.

It was not easy to make the decision to send American boys again into battle. I was a soldier in the First World War, and I know what a soldier goes through. I know well the anguish that mothers and fathers and families go through. So I knew what was ahead if we acted in Korea.

But after all this was said, we realized that the issue was whether there would be fighting in a limited area now or on a much larger scale later on—whether there would be some casualties now or many more casualties later.

So a decision was reached—the decision I believe was the most important in my time as President of the United States.

In the days that followed, the most heartening fact was that the American people clearly agreed with the decision.

And in Korea, our men are fighting as valiantly as Americans have ever fought—because they know they are fighting in the same cause of freedom in which Americans have stood ever since the beginning of the Republic.

Where free men had failed the test before, this time we met the test.

We met it firmly. We met it successfully. The aggression has been repelled. The Communists have seen their hopes of easy conquest go down the drain. The determination of free people to defend themselves has been made clear to the Kremlin.

As I have thought about our worldwide struggle with the Communists these past 8 years—day in and day out—I have never once doubted that you, the people of our country, have the will to do what is necessary to win this terrible fight against communism. I know the people of this country have that will and determination, and I have always depended on it. Because I have been sure of that, I have been able to make necessary decisions even though they called for sacrifices by all of us. And I have not been wrong in my judgment of the American people.

That same assurance of our people's determination will be General Eisenhower's greatest source of strength in carrying on this struggle.

Now, once in a while, I get a letter from some impatient person asking, why don't we get it over with? Why don't we issue an ultimatum, make all-out war, drop the atomic bomb?

For most Americans, the answer is quite simple: We are not made that way. We are a moral people. Peace is our goal, with justice and freedom. We cannot, of our own free will, violate the very principles that we are striving to defend. The whole purpose of what we are doing is to prevent world war III. Starting a war is no way to make peace.

But if anyone still thinks that just this once, bad means can bring good ends, then let me remind you of this: We are living in the 8th year of the atomic age. We are not the only nation that is learning to unleash the power of the atom. A third world war might dig the grave not only of our Communist opponents but also of our own society, our world as well as theirs.

Starting an atomic war is totally unthinkable for rational men.

Then, some of you may ask, when and how will the cold war end? I think I can answer that simply. The Communist world has great resources, and it looks strong. But there is a fatal flaw in their society. Theirs is a godless system, a system of slavery; there is no freedom in it, no consent. The Iron Curtain, the secret police, the constant purges, all these are symptoms of a great basic weakness—the rulers' fear of their own people.

In the long run the strength of our free society, and our ideals, will prevail over a system that has respect for neither God nor man.
Last week, in my State of the Union Message to the Congress—and I hope you will all take the time to read it—I explained how I think we will finally win through.

As the free world grows stronger, more united, more attractive to men on both sides of the Iron Curtain—and as the Soviet hopes for easy expansion are blocked—then there will have to come a time of change in the Soviet world. Nobody can say for sure when that is going to be, or exactly how it will come about, whether by revolution, or trouble in the satellite states, or by a change inside the Kremlin.

Whether the Communist rulers shift their policies of their own free will—or whether the change comes about in some other way—I have not a doubt in the world that a change will occur.

I have a deep and abiding faith in the destiny of free men. With patience and courage, we shall some day move on into a new era—a wonderful golden age—an age when we can use the peaceful tools that science has forged for us to do away with poverty and human misery everywhere on earth.

Think what can be done, once our capital, our skills, our science— most of all atomic energy—can be released from the tasks of defense and turned wholly to peaceful purposes all around the world.

There is no end to what can be done.

I can't help but dream out loud just a little here.

The Tigris and Euphrates Valley can be made to bloom as it did in the times of Babylon and Nineveh. Israel can be made the country of milk and honey as it was in the time of Joshua.

There is a plateau in Ethiopia some 6,000 to 8,000 feet high, that has 65,000 square miles of land just exactly like the corn belt in northern

Illinois. Enough food can be raised there to feed a hundred million people.

There are places in South America—places in Colombia and Venezuela and Brazil—just like that plateau in Ethiopia—places where food could be raised for millions of people.

These things can be done, and they are self-liquidating projects. If we can get peace and safety in the world under the United Nations, the developments will come so fast we will not recognize the world in which we now live.

This is our dream of the future—our picture of the world we hope to have when the Communist threat is overcome.

I've talked a lot tonight about the menace of communism—and our fight against it—because that is the overriding issue of our time. But there are some other things we've done that history will record. One of them is that we in America have learned how to attain real prosperity for our people.

We have 62 1/2 million people at work. Businessmen, farmers, laborers, white-collar people, all have better incomes and more of the good things of life than ever before in the history of the world.

There hasn't been a failure of an insured bank in nearly 9 years. No depositor has lost a cent in that period.

And the income of our people has been fairly distributed, perhaps more so than at any other time in recent history.

We have made progress in spreading the blessings of American life to all of our people. There has been a tremendous awakening of the American conscience on the great issues of civil rights—equal economic opportunities, equal rights of citizenship, and equal educational opportunities for all our people, whatever their race or religion or status of birth.

So, as I empty the drawers of this desk, and as Mrs. Truman and I leave the White House, we have no regret. We feel we have done our best in the public service. I hope and believe we have contributed to the welfare of this Nation and to the peace of the world.

When Franklin Roosevelt died, I felt there must be a million men better qualified than I, to take up the Presidential task. But the work was mine to do, and I had to do it. And I have tried to give it everything that was in me.

Through all of it, through all the years that I have worked here in this room, I have been well aware I did not really work alone—that you were working with me.

No President could ever hope to lead our country, or to sustain the burdens of this office, save as the people helped with their support. I have had that help—you have given me that support—on all our great essential undertakings to build the free world's strength and keep the peace.

Those are the big things. Those are the things we have done together.

For that I shall be grateful, always.

And now, the time has come for me to say good night—and God bless you all.

Dwight D. Eisenhower

FAREWELL ADDRESS
TUESDAY, JANUARY 17, 1961

On the evening of January 17, 1961, President Dwight D. Eisenhower made his farewell address from the Oval Office directly to the American people on television and radio. President Eisenhower's farewell address, in which he famously warned against the "military-industrial complex," is considered by many to be his most important speech.

My fellow Americans:

THREE DAYS FROM NOW, after half a century in the service of our country, I shall lay down the responsibilities of office as, in traditional and solemn ceremony, the authority of the Presidency is vested in my successor.

This evening I come to you with a message of leave-taking and farewell, and to share a few final thoughts with you, my countrymen.

Like every other citizen, I wish the new President, and all who will labor with him, Godspeed. I pray that the coming years will be blessed with peace and prosperity for all.

Our people expect their President and the Congress to find essential agreement on issues of great moment, the wise resolution of which will better shape the future of the Nation.

My own relations with the Congress, which began on a remote and tenuous basis when, long ago, a member of the Senate appointed me to West Point, have since ranged to the intimate during the war and immediate post-war period, and, finally, to the mutually interdependent during these past eight years.

In this final relationship, the Congress and the Administration have, on most vital issues, cooperated well, to serve the national good rather than mere partisanship, and so have assured that the business of the Nation should go forward. So, my official relationship with the Congress ends in a feeling, on my part, of gratitude that we have been able to do so much together.

II.

We now stand ten years past the midpoint of a century that has witnessed four major wars among great nations. Three of these involved our own country. Despite these holocausts America is today the strongest, the most influential and most productive nation in the world. Understandably proud of this pre-eminence, we yet realize that America's leadership and prestige depend, not merely upon our unmatched material progress, riches and military strength, but on how we use our power in the interests of world peace and human betterment.

III.

Throughout America's adventure in free government, our basic purposes have been to keep the peace; to foster progress in human achievement, and to enhance liberty, dignity and integrity among people and among nations. To strive for less would be unworthy of a free and religious people. Any failure traceable to arrogance, or our lack of comprehension or readiness to sacrifice would inflict upon us grievous hurt both at home and abroad.

Progress toward these noble goals is persistently threatened by the conflict now engulfing the world. It commands our whole attention, absorbs our very beings. We face a hostile ideology—global in scope, atheistic in character, ruthless in purpose, and insidious in method. Unhappily the danger it poses promises to be of indefinite duration. To meet it successfully, there is called for, not so much the emotional and transitory sacrifices of crisis, but rather those which enable us to carry forward steadily, surely, and without complaint the burdens of a prolonged and complex struggle—with liberty the stake. Only thus shall we remain, despite every provocation, on our charted course toward permanent peace and human betterment.

Crises there will continue to be. In meeting them, whether foreign or domestic, great or small, there is a recurring temptation to feel that some spectacular and costly action could become the miraculous solution to all current difficulties. A huge increase in newer elements of our defense; development of unrealistic programs to cure every ill in agriculture; a dramatic expansion in basic and applied research—these and many other possibilities, each possibly promising in itself, may be suggested as the only way to the road we wish to travel.

But each proposal must be weighed in the light of a broader consideration: the need to maintain balance in and among national programs—balance between the private and the public economy, balance between cost and hoped for advantage—balance between the clearly necessary and the comfortably desirable; balance between our essential requirements as a nation and the duties imposed by the nation upon the individual; balance between actions of the moment and the national welfare of the future. Good judgment seeks balance and progress; lack of it eventually finds imbalance and frustration.

The record of many decades stands as proof that our people and their government have, in the main, understood these truths and have responded to them well, in the face of stress and threat. But threats, new in kind or degree, constantly arise. I mention two only.

IV.

A vital element in keeping the peace is our military establishment. Our arms must be mighty, ready for instant action, so that no potential aggressor may be tempted to risk his own destruction.

Our military organization today bears little relation to that known by any of my predecessors in peacetime, or indeed by the fighting men of World War II or Korea.

Until the latest of our world conflicts, the United States had no armaments industry. American makers of plowshares could, with time and as required, make swords as well. But now we can no longer risk emergency improvisation of national defense; we have been compelled to create a permanent armaments industry of vast proportions. Added to this, three and a half million men and women are directly engaged in the defense establishment. We annually spend on military security more than the net income of all United States corporations.

This conjunction of an immense military establishment and a large arms industry is new in the American experience. The total influence—economic, political, even spiritual—is felt in every city, every State house, every office of the Federal government. We recognize the imperative need for this development. Yet we must not fail to comprehend its grave implications. Our toil, resources and livelihood are all involved; so is the very structure of our society.

In the councils of government, we must guard against the acquisition of unwarranted influence, whether sought or unsought, by the military-industrial complex. The potential for the disastrous rise of misplaced power exists and will persist.

We must never let the weight of this combination endanger our liberties or democratic processes. We should take nothing for granted. Only an alert and knowledgeable citizenry can compel the proper meshing of the huge industrial and military machinery of defense with our peaceful methods and goals, so that security and liberty may prosper together.

Akin to, and largely responsible for the sweeping changes in our industrial-military posture, has been the technological revolution during recent decades.

In this revolution, research has become central; it also becomes more formalized, complex, and costly. A steadily increasing share is conducted for, by, or at the direction of, the Federal government.

Today, the solitary inventor, tinkering in his shop, has been overshadowed by task forces of scientists in laboratories and testing fields. In the same fashion, the free university, historically the fountainhead of free ideas and scientific discovery, has experienced a revolution in the conduct of research. Partly because of the huge costs involved, a government contract becomes virtually a substitute for intellectual curiosity. For every old blackboard there are now hundreds of new electronic computers.

The prospect of domination of the nation's scholars by Federal employment, project allocations, and the power of money is ever present— and is gravely to be regarded.

Yet, in holding scientific research and discovery in respect, as we should, we must also be alert to the equal and opposite danger that public policy could itself become the captive of a scientific-technological elite.

It is the task of statesmanship to mold, to balance, and to integrate these and other forces, new and old, within the principles of our democratic system—ever aiming toward the supreme goals of our free society.

V.

Another factor in maintaining balance involves the element of time. As we peer into society's future, we—you and I, and our government—must avoid the impulse to live only for today, plundering, for our own ease and convenience, the precious resources of tomorrow. We cannot mortgage the material assets of our grandchildren without risking the loss also of their political and spiritual heritage. We want democracy to survive for all generations to come, not to become the insolvent phantom of tomorrow.

VI.

Down the long lane of the history yet to be written America knows that this world of ours, ever growing smaller, must avoid becoming a community of dreadful fear and hate, and be, instead, a proud confederation of mutual trust and respect.

Such a confederation must be one of equals. The weakest must come to the conference table with the same confidence as do we, protected as we are by our moral, economic, and military strength. That table, though scarred by many past frustrations, cannot be abandoned for the certain agony of the battlefield.

Disarmament, with mutual honor and confidence, is a continuing imperative. Together we must learn how to compose differences, not with arms, but with intellect and decent purpose. Because this need is so sharp and apparent I confess that I lay down my official responsibilities in this field with a definite sense of disappointment. As one who has witnessed the horror and the lingering sadness of war—as one who knows that another war could utterly destroy this civilization which has been so slowly and painfully built over thousands of years—I wish I could say tonight that a lasting peace is in sight.

Happily, I can say that war has been avoided. Steady progress toward our ultimate goal has been made. But, so much remains to be done. As a private citizen, I shall never cease to do what little I can to help the world advance along that road.

VII.

So—in this my last good night to you as your President—I thank you for the many opportunities you have given me for public service in war and peace. I trust that in that service you find some things worthy; as for the rest of it, I know you will find ways to improve performance in the future.

You and I—my fellow citizens—need to be strong in our faith that all nations, under God, will reach the goal of peace with justice. May we be ever unswerving in devotion to principle, confident but humble with power, diligent in pursuit of the Nation's great goals.

To all the peoples of the world, I once more give expression to America's prayerful and continuing aspiration:

We pray that peoples of all faiths, all races, all nations, may have their great human needs satisfied; that those now denied opportunity shall come to enjoy it to the full; that all who yearn for freedom may experience its spiritual blessings; that those who have freedom will understand, also, its heavy responsibilities; that all who are insensitive to the needs of others will learn charity; that the scourges of poverty, disease and ignorance will be made to disappear from the earth, and that, in the goodness of time, all peoples will come to live together in a peace guaranteed by the binding force of mutual respect and love.

JIMMY CARTER

FAREWELL ADDRESS
WEDNESDAY, JANUARY 14, 1981

In the shadow of an ongoing Iran hostage crisis, President Jimmy Carter addressed the nation via radio and television on the evening of January 14, 1981. President Carter hoped to instill again in a "doubtful" American people the ideals of the Declaration of Independence—"For this generation, ours, life is nuclear survival; liberty is human rights; the pursuit of happiness is a planet whose resources are devoted to the physical and spiritual nourishment of its inhabitants."

GOOD EVENING. In a few days I will lay down my official responsibilities in this office, to take up once more the only title in our democracy superior to that of President, the title of citizen.

Of Vice President Mondale, my Cabinet, and the hundreds of others who have served with me during the last 4 years, I wish to say now publicly what I have said in private: I thank them for the dedication and competence they've brought to the service of our country. But I owe my deepest thanks to you, to the American people, because you gave me this extraordinary opportunity to serve.

We've faced great challenges together, and we know that future problems will also be difficult. But I'm now more convinced than ever that the United States, better than any other country, can meet successfully whatever the future might bring. These last 4 years have made me more certain than ever of the inner strength of our country, the unchanging value of our principles and ideals, the stability of our political system, the ingenuity and the decency of our people.

Tonight I would like first to say a few words about this most special office, the Presidency of the United States. This is at once the most powerful office in the world and among the most severely constrained by law and custom. The President is given a broad responsibility to lead but cannot do so without the support and consent of the people, expressed formally through the Congress and informally in many ways through a whole range of public and private institutions. This is as it should be.

Within our system of government every American has a right and a duty to help shape the future course of the United States. Thoughtful criticism and close scrutiny of all government officials by the press and the public are an important part of our democratic society. Now, as in the past, only the understanding and involvement of the people through full and open debate can help to avoid serious mistakes and assure the continued dignity and safety of the Nation.

Today we are asking our political system to do things of which the Founding Fathers never dreamed. The government they designed for a few hundred thousand people now serves a nation of almost 230 million people. Their small coastal republic now spans beyond a continent, and we also now have the responsibility to help lead much of the world through difficult times to a secure and prosperous future.

Today, as people have become ever more doubtful of the ability of the Government to deal with our problems, we are increasingly drawn to single-issue groups and special interest organizations to ensure that whatever else happens, our own personal views and our own private interests are protected. This is a disturbing factor in American political life. It tends to distort our purposes, because the national interest is not always the sum of all our single or special interests. We are all Americans together, and we must not forget that the common good is our common interest and our individual responsibility.

Because of the fragmented pressures of these special interests, it's very important that the office of the President be a strong one and that its constitutional authority be preserved. The President is the only elected official charged with the primary responsibility of representing all the people. In the moments of decision, after the different and conflicting views have all been aired, it's the President who then must speak to the Nation and for the Nation.

I understand after 4 years in this office, as few others can, how formidable is the task the new President-elect is about to undertake, and to the very limits of conscience and conviction, I pledge to support him in that task. I wish him success, and Godspeed.

I know from experience that Presidents have to face major issues that are controversial, broad in scope, and which do not arouse the natural support of a political majority. For a few minutes now, I want to lay aside my role as leader of one nation, and speak to you as a fellow citizen of the world about three issues, three difficult issues: the threat of nuclear destruction, our stewardship of the physical resources of our planet, and the preeminence of the basic rights of human beings.

It's now been 35 years since the first atomic bomb fell on Hiroshima. The great majority of the world's people cannot remember a time when the nuclear shadow did not hang over the Earth. Our minds have adjusted to it, as after a time our eyes adjust to the dark. Yet the risk of a nuclear conflagration has not lessened. It has not happened yet, thank God, but that can give us little comfort, for it only has to happen once.

The danger is becoming greater. As the arsenals of the superpowers grow in size and sophistication and as other governments, perhaps even in the future dozens of governments, acquire these weapons, it may only be a matter of time before madness, desperation, greed, or miscalculation lets loose this terrible force.

In an all-out nuclear war, more destructive power than in all of World War II would be unleashed every second during the long afternoon it would take for all the missiles and bombs to fall. A World War II every second—more people killed in the first few hours than in all the wars of history put together. The survivors, if any, would live in despair amid the poisoned ruins of a civilization that had committed suicide.

National weakness, real or perceived, can tempt aggression and thus cause war. That's why the United States can never neglect its military strength. We must and we will remain strong. But with equal determination, the United States and all countries must find ways to control and to reduce the horrifying danger that is posed by the enormous world stockpiles of nuclear arms.

This has been a concern of every American President since the moment we first saw what these weapons could do. Our leaders will require our understanding and our support as they grapple with this difficult but crucial challenge. There is no disagreement on the goals or the basic approach to controlling this enormous destructive force. The answer lies not just in the attitudes or the actions of world leaders but in the concern and the demands of all of us as we continue our struggle to preserve the peace.

Nuclear weapons are an expression of one side of our human character. But there's another side. The same rocket technology that delivers nuclear warheads has also taken us peacefully into space. From that perspective, we see our Earth as it really is—a small and fragile and beautiful blue globe, the only home we have. We see no barriers of race or religion or country. We see the essential unity of our species and our planet. And with faith and common sense, that bright vision will ultimately prevail.

Another major challenge, therefore, is to protect the quality of this world within which we live. The shadows that fall across the future are cast not only by the kinds of weapons we've built, but by the kind of world we will either nourish or neglect. There are real and growing dangers to our simple and our most precious possessions: the air we breathe, the water we drink, and the land which sustains us. The rapid depletion of irreplaceable minerals, the erosion of topsoil, the destruction of beauty, the blight of pollution, the demands of increasing billions of people, all combine to create problems which are easy to observe and predict, but difficult to resolve. If we do not act, the world of the year 2000 will be much less able to sustain life than it is now.

But there is no reason for despair. Acknowledging the physical realities of our planet does not mean a dismal future of endless sacrifice. In fact, acknowledging these realities is the first step in dealing with them. We can meet the resource problems of the world—water, food, minerals, farmlands, forests, overpopulation, pollution if we tackle them with courage and foresight.

I've just been talking about forces of potential destruction that mankind has developed and how we might control them. It's equally important that we remember the beneficial forces that we have evolved over the ages and how to hold fast to them. One of those constructive forces is the enhancement of individual human freedoms through the strengthening of democracy and the fight against deprivation, torture, terrorism, and the persecution of people throughout the world. The struggle for human rights overrides all differences of color or nation or language. Those who hunger for freedom, who thirst for human dignity, and who suffer for the sake of justice, they are the patriots of this cause.

I believe with all my heart that America must always stand for these basic human rights at home and abroad. That is both our history and our destiny.

America did not invent human rights. In a very real sense, it's the other way around. Human rights invented America. Ours was the first nation in the history of the world to be founded explicitly on such an idea. Our social and political progress has been based on one fundamental principle: the value and importance of the individual. The fundamental force that unites us is not kinship or place of origin or religious preference. The love of liberty is the common blood that flows in our American veins.

The battle for human rights, at home and abroad, is far from over. We should never be surprised nor discouraged, because the impact of our efforts has had and will always have varied results. Rather, we should take pride that the ideals which gave birth to our Nation still inspire the hopes of oppressed people around the world. We have no cause for self-righteousness or complacency, but we have every reason to persevere, both within our own country and beyond our borders.

If we are to serve as a beacon for human rights, we must continue to perfect here at home the rights and the values which we espouse around the world: a decent education for our children, adequate medical care for all Americans, an end to discrimination against minorities and women, a job for all those able to work, and freedom from injustice and religious intolerance.

We live in a time of transition, an uneasy era which is likely to endure for the rest of this century. It will be a period of tensions, both within nations and between nations, of competition for scarce resources, of social, political, and economic stresses and strains. During this period we may be tempted to abandon some of the time-honored principles and commitments which have been proven during the difficult times of past generations. We must never yield to this temptation. Our American values are not luxuries, but necessities—not the salt in our bread, but the bread itself. Our common vision of a free and just society is our greatest source of cohesion at home and strength abroad, greater even than the bounty of our material blessings.

Remember these words: "We hold these truths to be self-evident, that all men are created equal, that they are endowed by their Creator with certain inalienable Rights, that among these are Life, Liberty and the pursuit of Happiness."

This vision still grips the imagination of the world. But we know that democracy is always an unfinished creation. Each generation must renew its foundations. Each generation must rediscover the meaning of this hallowed vision in the light of its own modern challenges. For this generation, ours, life is nuclear survival; liberty is human rights; the pursuit of happiness is a planet whose resources are devoted to the physical and spiritual nourishment of its inhabitants.

During the next few days I will work hard to make sure that the transition from myself to the next President is a good one, that the American people are served well. And I will continue, as I have the last 14 months, to work hard and to pray for the lives and the well-being of the American hostages held in Iran. I can't predict yet what will happen, but I hope you will join me in my constant prayer for their freedom.

As I return home to the South, where I was born and raised, I look forward to the opportunity to reflect and further to assess, I hope with accuracy, the circumstances of our times. I intend to give our new President my support, and I intend to work as a citizen, as I've worked here in this office as President, for the values this Nation was founded to secure.

Again, from the bottom of my heart, I want to express to you the gratitude I feel. Thank you, fellow citizens, and farewell.

Ronald Reagan

FAREWELL ADDRESS
WEDNESDAY, JANUARY 11, 1989

On January 11, 1989, Ronald Reagan gave his final address to the American people. Televised from the Oval Office, the "Great Communicator," as he was known, spoke plainly to the American people. After eight years of a presidency that saw a resurgence of national pride and patriotism, President Reagan warned, "This national feeling is good, but it won't count for much, and it won't last unless it's grounded in thoughtfulness and knowledge."

THIS IS THE 34th TIME I'll speak to you from the Oval Office, and the last. We've been together eight years now, and soon it'll be time for me to go. But before I do, I wanted to share some thoughts, some of which I've been saving for a long time.

It's been the honor of my life to be your President. So many of you have written the past few weeks to say thanks, but I could say as much to you. Nancy and I are grateful for the opportunity you gave us to serve.

One of the things about the Presidency is that you're always somewhat apart. You spent a lot of time going by too fast in a car someone else is driving, and seeing the people through tinted glass—the parents holding up a child, and the wave you saw too late and couldn't return. And so many times I wanted to stop and reach out from behind the glass, and connect. Well, maybe I can do a little of that tonight.

People ask how I feel about leaving. And the fact is, "parting is such sweet sorrow." The sweet part is California and the ranch and freedom. The sorrow—the goodbyes, of course, and leaving this beautiful place.

You know, down the hall and up the stairs from this office is the part of the White House where the President and his family live. There are a few favorite windows I have up there that I like to stand and look out of early in the morning. The view is over the grounds here to the Washington Monument, and then the Mall and the Jefferson Memorial. But on mornings when the humidity is low, you can see past the Jefferson to the river, the Potomac, and the Virginia shore. Someone said that's the view Lincoln had when he saw the smoke rising from the Battle of Bull Run. I see more prosaic things: the grass on the banks, the morning traffic as people make their way to work, now and then a sailboat on the river.

I've been thinking a bit at that window. I've been reflecting on what the past eight years have meant and mean. And the image that comes to mind like a refrain is a nautical one—a small story about a big ship, and a refugee, and a sailor. It was back in the early '80s, at the height of the boat people. And the sailor was hard at work on the carrier *Midway*, which was patrolling the South China Sea. The sailor, like most American servicemen, was young, smart, and fiercely observant. The crew spied on the horizon a leaky little boat. And crammed inside were refugees from Indochina hoping to get to America. The *Midway* sent a small launch to bring them to the ship and safety. As the refugees made their way through the choppy seas, one spied the sailor on deck, and stood up, and called out to him. He yelled, "Hello, American sailor. Hello, freedom man."

A small moment with a big meaning, a moment the sailor, who wrote it in a letter, couldn't get out of his mind. And, when I saw it, neither could I. Because that's what it was to be an American in the 1980s. We stood, again, for freedom. I know we always have, but in the past few years the world again—and in a way, we ourselves—rediscovered it.

It's been quite a journey this decade, and we held together through some stormy seas. And at the end, together, we are reaching our destination.

The fact is, from Grenada to the Washington and Moscow summits, from the recession of '81 to '82, to the expansion that began in late '82 and continues to this day, we've made a difference. The way I see it, there were two great triumphs, two things that I'm proudest of. One is the economic recovery, in which the people of America created—and filled—19 million new jobs. The other is the recovery of our morale. America is respected again in the world and looked to for leadership.

Something that happened to me a few years ago reflects some of this. It was back in 1981, and I was attending my first big economic summit, which was held that year in Canada. The meeting place rotates among the member countries. The opening meeting was a formal dinner of the heads of government of the seven industrialized nations. Now, I sat there like the new kid in school and listened, and it was all Francois this and Helmut that. They dropped titles and spoke to one another on a first-name basis. Well, at one point I sort of leaned in and said, "My name's Ron." Well, in that same year, we began the actions we felt would ignite an economic comeback—cut taxes and regulation, started to cut spending. And soon the recovery began.

Two years later, another economic summit with pretty much the same cast. At the big opening meeting we all got together, and all of a sudden, just for a moment, I saw that everyone was just sitting there looking at me. And then one of them broke the silence. "Tell us about the American miracle," he said.

Well, back in 1980, when I was running for President, it was all so different. Some pundits said our programs would result in catastrophe. Our views on foreign affairs would cause war. Our plans for the economy would cause inflation to soar and bring about economic collapse. I even remember one highly respected economist saying, back in 1982, that "the engines of economic growth have shut down here, and they're likely to stay that way for years to come." Well, he and the other opinion leaders were wrong. The fact is what they call "radical" was really "right." What they called "dangerous" was just "desperately needed."

And in all of that time I won a nickname, "The Great Communicator." But I never thought it was my style or the words I used that made a difference: it was the content. I wasn't a great communicator, but I communicated great things, and they didn't spring full bloom from my brow, they came from the heart of a great nation—from our experience, our wisdom, and our belief in the principles that have guided us for two centuries. They called it the Reagan revolution. Well, I'll accept that, but for me it always seemed more like the great rediscovery, a rediscovery of our values and our common sense.

Common sense told us that when you put a big tax on something, the people will produce less of it. So, we cut the people's tax rates, and the people produced more than ever before. The economy bloomed like a plant that had been cut back and could now grow quicker and stronger. Our economic program brought about the longest peacetime expansion in our history: real family income up, the poverty rate down, entrepreneurship booming, and an explosion in research and new technology. We're exporting more than ever because American industry became more competitive and at the same time, we summoned the national will to knock down protectionist walls abroad instead of erecting them at home.

Common sense also told us that to preserve the peace, we'd have to become strong again after years of weakness and confusion. So, we rebuilt our defenses, and this New Year we toasted the new peacefulness around the globe. Not only have the superpowers actually begun to reduce their stockpiles of nuclear weapons—and hope for even more progress is bright—but the regional conflicts that rack the globe are also beginning to cease. The Persian Gulf is no longer a war zone. The Soviets are leaving Afghanistan. The Vietnamese are preparing to pull out of Cambodia, and an American-mediated accord will soon send 50,000 Cuban troops home from Angola.

The lesson of all this was, of course, that because we're a great nation, our challenges seem complex. It will always be this way. But as long as we remember our first principles and believe in ourselves, the future will always be ours. And something else we learned: Once you begin a great movement, there's no telling where it will end. We meant to change a nation, and instead, we changed a world.

Countries across the globe are turning to free markets and free speech and turning away from the ideologies of the past. For them, the great rediscovery of the 1980s has been that, lo and behold, the moral way of government is the practical way of government: Democracy, the profoundly good, is also the profoundly productive.

When you've got to the point when you can celebrate the anniversaries of your 39th birthday you can sit back sometimes, review your life, and see it flowing before you. For me there was a fork in the river, and it was right in the middle of my life. I never meant to go into politics. It wasn't my intention when I was young. But I was raised to believe you had to pay your way for the blessings bestowed on you. I was happy with my career in the entertainment world, but I ultimately went into politics because I wanted to protect something precious.

Ours was the first revolution in the history of mankind that truly reversed the course of government, and with three little words: "We the People." "We the People" tell the government what to do; it doesn't tell us. "We the People" are the driver; the government is the car. And we decide where it should go, and by what route, and how fast. Almost all the world's constitutions are documents in which governments tell the people what their privileges are. Our Constitution is a document in which "We the People" tell the government what it is allowed to do. "We the People" are free. This belief has been the underlying basis for everything I've tried to do these past eight years.

But back in the 1960s, when I began, it seemed to me that we'd begun reversing the order of things—that through more and more rules and regulations and confiscatory taxes, the government was taking more of our money, more of our options, and more of our freedom. I went into politics in part to put up my hand and say, "Stop." I was a citizen politician, and it seemed the right thing for a citizen to do.

I think we have stopped a lot of what needed stopping. And I hope we have once again reminded people that man is not free unless government is limited. There's a clear cause and effect here that is as neat and predictable as a law of physics: As government expands, liberty contracts.

Nothing is less free than pure Communism—and yet we have, the past few years, forged a satisfying new closeness with the Soviet Union. I've been asked if this isn't a gamble, and my answer is no because we're basing our actions not on words but deeds. The detente of the 1970s was based not on actions but promises. They'd promise to treat their own people and the people of the world better. But the gulag was still the gulag, and the state was still expansionist, and they still waged proxy wars in Africa, Asia, and Latin America.

Well, this time, so far, it's different. President Gorbachev has brought about some internal democratic reforms and begun the withdrawal from Afghanistan. He has also freed prisoners whose names I've given him every time we've met.

But life has a way of reminding you of big things through small incidents. Once, during the heady days of the Moscow summit, Nancy and I decided to break off from the entourage one afternoon to visit the shops on Arbat Street—that's a little street just off Moscow's main shopping area. Even though our visit was a surprise, every Russian there immediately recognized us and called out our names and reached for our hands. We were just about swept away by the warmth. You could almost feel the possibilities in all that joy. But within seconds, a KGB detail pushed their way toward us and began pushing and shoving the people in the crowd. It was an interesting moment. It reminded me that while the man on the street in the Soviet Union yearns for peace, the government is Communist. And those who run it are Communists, and that means we and they view such issues as freedom and human rights very differently.

We must keep up our guard, but we must also continue to work together to lessen and eliminate tension and mistrust. My view is that President Gorbachev is different from previous Soviet leaders. I think he knows some of the things wrong with his society and is trying to fix them. We wish him well. And we'll continue to work to make sure that the Soviet Union that eventually emerges from this process is a less threatening one. What it all boils down to is this: I want the new closeness to continue. And it will, as long as we make it clear that we will continue to act in a certain way as long as they continue to act in a helpful manner. If and when they don't, at first pull your punches. If they persist, pull the plug. It's still trust but verify. It's still play, but cut the cards. It's still watch closely. And don't be afraid to see what you see.

I've been asked if I have any regrets. Well, I do. The deficit is one. I've been talking a great deal about that lately, but tonight isn't for arguments, and I'm going to hold my tongue. But an observation: I've had my share of victories in the Congress, but what few people noticed is that I never won anything you didn't win for me. They never saw my troops, they never saw Reagan's regiments, the American people. You won every battle with every call you made and letter you wrote demanding action. Well, action is still needed. If we're to finish the job, Reagan's regiments will have to become the Bush brigades. Soon he'll be the chief, and he'll need you every bit as much as I did.

Finally, there is a great tradition of warnings in Presidential farewells, and I've got one that's been on my mind for some time. But oddly enough it starts with one of the things I'm proudest of in the past eight years: the resurgence of national pride that I called the new patriotism. This national feeling is good, but it won't count for much, and it won't last unless it's grounded in thoughtfulness and knowledge.

An informed patriotism is what we want. And are we doing a good enough job teaching our children what America is and what she represents in the long history of the world? Those of us who are over 35 or so years of age grew up in a different America. We were taught, very directly, what it means to be an American. And we absorbed, almost in the air, a love of country and an appreciation of its institutions. If you didn't get these things from your family you got them from the neighborhood, from the father down the street who fought in Korea or the family who lost someone at Anzio. Or you could get a sense of patriotism from school. And if all else failed you could get a sense of patriotism from the popular culture. The movies celebrated democratic values and implicitly reinforced the idea that America was special. TV was like that, too, through the mid-'60s.

But now, we're about to enter the '90s, and some things have changed. Younger parents aren't sure that an unambivalent appreciation of America is the right thing to teach modern children. And as for those who create the popular culture, well-grounded patriotism is no longer the style. Our spirit is back, but we haven't reinstitutionalized it. We've got to do a better job of getting across that America is freedom—freedom of speech, freedom of religion, freedom of enterprise. And freedom is special and rare. It's fragile; it needs protection.

So, we've got to teach history based not on what's in fashion but what's important—why the Pilgrims came here, who Jimmy Doolittle was, and what those 30 seconds over Tokyo meant. You know, four years ago on the 40th anniversary of D-Day, I read a letter from a young woman writing to her late father, who'd fought on Omaha Beach. Her name was Lisa Zanatta Henn, and she said, "we will always remember, we will never forget what the boys of Normandy did." Well, let's help her keep her word. If we forget what we did, we won't know who we are. I'm warning of an eradication of the American memory that could result, ultimately, in an erosion of the American spirit. Let's start with some basics: more attention to American history and a greater emphasis on civic ritual.

And let me offer lesson number one about America: All great change in America begins at the dinner table. So, tomorrow night in the kitchen I hope the talking begins. And children, if your parents haven't been teaching you what it means to be an American, let 'em know and nail 'em on it. That would be a very American thing to do.

And that's about all I have to say tonight, except for one thing. The past few days when I've been at that window upstairs, I've thought a bit of the "shining city upon a hill." The phrase comes from John Winthrop, who wrote it to describe the America he imagined. What he imagined was important because he was an early Pilgrim, an early freedom man. He journeyed here on what today we'd call a little wooden boat; and like the other Pilgrims, he was looking for a home that would be free. I've spoken of the shining city all my political life, but I don't know if I ever quite communicated what I saw when I said it. But in my mind it was a tall, proud city built on rocks stronger than oceans, windswept, God-blessed, and teeming with people of all kinds living in harmony and peace; a city with free ports that hummed with commerce and creativity. And if there had to be city walls, the walls had doors and the doors were open to anyone with the will and the heart to get here. That's how I saw it, and see it still.

And how stands the city on this winter night? More prosperous, more secure, and happier than it was eight years ago. But more than that: After 200 years, two centuries, she still stands strong and true on the granite ridge, and her glow has held steady no matter what storm. And she's still a beacon, still a magnet for all who must have freedom, for all the pilgrims from all the lost places who are hurtling through the darkness, toward home.

We've done our part. And as I walk off into the city streets, a final word to the men and women of the Reagan revolution, the men and women across America who for eight years did the work that brought America back. My friends: We did it. We weren't just marking time. We made a difference. We made the city stronger, we made the city freer, and we left her in good hands. All in all, not bad, not bad at all.

And so, goodbye, God bless you, and God bless the United States of America.

WILLIAM JEFFERSON CLINTON

FAREWELL ADDRESS
THURSDAY, JANUARY 18, 2001

On January 18, 2001, President Clinton made his farewell address from the Oval Office to his "Fellow Citizens." The seven-minute speech focused on issues of fiscal responsibility, social progress, and America's leadership role in the world. "In his first Inaugural Address, Thomas Jefferson warned of entangling alliances. But in our times, America cannot and must not disentangle itself from the world."

MY FELLOW CITIZENS, tonight is my last opportunity to speak to you from the Oval Office as your President. I am profoundly grateful to you for twice giving me the honor to serve, to work for you and with you to prepare our Nation for the 21st century.

And I'm grateful to Vice President Gore, to my Cabinet Secretaries, and to all those who have served with me for the last eight years.

This has been a time of dramatic transformation, and you have risen to every new challenge. You have made our social fabric stronger, our families healthier and safer, our people more prosperous. You, the American people, have made our passage into the global information age an era of great American renewal.

In all the work I have done as President—every decision I have made, every executive action I have taken, every bill I have proposed and signed—I've tried to give all Americans the tools and conditions to build the future of our dreams in a good society with a strong economy, a cleaner environment, and a freer, safer, more prosperous world.

I have steered my course by our enduring values: opportunity for all, responsibility from all, a community of all Americans. I have sought to give America a new kind of Government, smaller, more modern, more effective, full of ideas and policies appropriate to this new time, always putting people first, always focusing on the future.

Working together, America has done well. Our economy is breaking records with more than 22 million new jobs, the lowest unemployment in 30 years, the highest homeownership ever, the longest expansion in history. Our families and communities are stronger. Thirty-five million Americans have used the family leave law; 8 million have moved off welfare. Crime is at a 25-year low. Over 10 million Americans receive more college aid, and more people than ever are going to college.

Our schools are better. Higher standards, greater accountability, and larger investments have brought higher test scores and higher graduation rates. More than 3 million children have health insurance now, and more than 7 million Americans have been lifted out of poverty. Incomes are rising across the board. Our air and water are cleaner. Our food and drinking water are safer. And more of our precious land has been preserved in the continental United States than at any time in 100 years.

America has been a force for peace and prosperity in every corner of the globe. I'm very grateful to be able to turn over the reins of leadership to a new President with America in such a strong position to meet the challenges of the future.

Tonight I want to leave you with three thoughts about our future. First, America must maintain our record of fiscal responsibility.

Through our last four budgets we've turned record deficits to record surpluses, and we've been able to pay down $600 billion of our national debt—on track to be debt-free by the end of the decade for the first time since 1835. Staying on that course will bring lower interest rates, greater prosperity, and the opportunity to meet our big challenges. If we choose wisely, we can pay down the debt, deal with the retirement of the baby boomers, invest more in our future, and provide tax relief.

Second, because the world is more connected every day, in every way, America's security and prosperity require us to continue to lead in the world. At this remarkable moment in history, more people live in freedom than ever before. Our alliances are stronger than ever. People all around the world look to America to be a force for peace and prosperity, freedom and security.

The global economy is giving more of our own people and billions around the world the chance to work and live and raise their families with dignity. But the forces of integration that have created these good opportunities also make us more subject to global forces of destruction, to terrorism, organized crime and narcotrafficking, the spread of deadly weapons and disease, the degradation of the global environment.

The expansion of trade hasn't fully closed the gap between those of us who live on the cutting edge of the global economy and the billions around the world who live on the knife's edge of survival. This global gap requires more than compassion; it requires action. Global poverty is a powder keg that could be ignited by our indifference.

In his first Inaugural Address, Thomas Jefferson warned of entangling alliances. But in our times, America cannot and must not disentangle itself from the world. If we want the world to embody our shared values, then we must assume a shared responsibility.

If the wars of the 20th century, especially the recent ones in Kosovo and Bosnia, have taught us anything, it is that we achieve our aims by defending our values and leading the forces of freedom and peace. We must embrace boldly and resolutely that duty to lead—to stand with our allies in word and deed and to put a human face on the global economy, so that expanded trade benefits all peoples in all nations, lifting lives and hopes all across the world.

Third, we must remember that America cannot lead in the world unless here at home we weave the threads of our coat of many colors into the fabric of one America. As we become ever more diverse, we must work harder to unite around our common values and our common humanity. We must work harder to overcome our differences, in our hearts and in our laws. We must treat all our people with fairness and dignity, regardless of their race, religion, gender, or sexual orientation, and regardless of when they arrived in our country—always moving toward the more perfect Union of our Founders' dreams.

Hillary, Chelsea, and I join all Americans in wishing our very best to the next President, George W. Bush, to his family and his administration, in meeting these challenges, and in leading freedom's march in this new century.

As for me, I'll leave the Presidency more idealistic, more full of hope than the day I arrived, and more confident than ever that America's best days lie ahead.

My days in this office are nearly through, but my days of service, I hope, are not. In the years ahead, I will never hold a position higher or a covenant more sacred than that of President of the United States. But there is no title I will wear more proudly than that of citizen.

Thank you. God bless you, and God bless America.

GEORGE W. BUSH

FAREWELL ADDRESS
THURSDAY, JANUARY 15, 2009

On January 15, 2009, President George W. Bush gave his farewell address. Departing from the tradition of past presidents, he gave his short, televised speech in the East Room of the White House in front of a live audience of courageous and compassionate people who had inspired him in the previous eight years. He warned that America's greatest threat was from a terrorist attack, while at the same time the nation must reject isolationism and protectionsim.

Fellow citizens:

FOR EIGHT YEARS, it has been my honor to serve as your President. The first decade of this new century has been a period of consequence—a time set apart. Tonight, with a thankful heart, I have asked for a final opportunity to share some thoughts on the journey that we have traveled together, and the future of our nation.

Five days from now, the world will witness the vitality of American democracy. In a tradition dating back to our founding, the presidency will pass to a successor chosen by you, the American people. Standing on the steps of the Capitol will be a man whose history reflects the enduring promise of our land. This is a moment of hope and pride for our whole nation. And I join all Americans in offering best wishes to President-Elect Obama, his wife Michelle, and their two beautiful girls.

Tonight I am filled with gratitude—to Vice President Cheney and members of my administration; to Laura, who brought joy to this house and love to my life; to our wonderful daughters, Barbara and Jenna; to my parents, whose examples have provided strength for a lifetime. And above all, I thank the American people for the trust you have given me. I thank you for the prayers that have lifted my spirits. And I thank you for the countless acts of courage, generosity, and grace that I have witnessed these past eight years.

This evening, my thoughts return to the first night I addressed you from this house—September the 11th, 2001. That morning, terrorists took nearly 3,000 lives in the worst attack on America since Pearl Harbor. I remember standing in the rubble of the World Trade Center three days later, surrounded by rescuers who had been working around the clock. I remember talking to brave souls who charged through smoke-filled corridors at the

Pentagon, and to husbands and wives whose loved ones became heroes aboard Flight 93. I remember Arlene Howard, who gave me her fallen son's police shield as a reminder of all that was lost. And I still carry his badge.

As the years passed, most Americans were able to return to life much as it had been before 9/11. But I never did. Every morning, I received a briefing on the threats to our nation. I vowed to do everything in my power to keep us safe.

Over the past seven years, a new Department of Homeland Security has been created. The military, the intelligence community, and the FBI have been transformed. Our nation is equipped with new tools to monitor the terrorists' movements, freeze their finances, and break up their plots. And with strong allies at our side, we have taken the fight to the terrorists and those who support them. Afghanistan has gone from a nation where the Taliban harbored al-Qaeda and stoned women in the streets to a young democracy that is fighting terror and encouraging girls to go to school. Iraq has gone from a brutal dictatorship and a sworn enemy of America to an Arab democracy at the heart of the Middle East and a friend of the United States.

There is legitimate debate about many of these decisions. But there can be little debate about the results. America has gone more than seven years without another terrorist attack on our soil. This is a tribute to those who toil night and day to keep us safe—law enforcement officers, intelligence analysts, homeland security and diplomatic personnel, and the men and women of the United States Armed Forces.

Our nation is blessed to have citizens who volunteer to defend us in this time of danger. I have cherished meeting these selfless patriots and their families. And America owes you a debt of gratitude. And to all our men and women in uniform listening tonight: There has been no higher honor than serving as your Commander-in-Chief.

The battles waged by our troops are part of a broader struggle between two dramatically different systems. Under one, a small band of fanatics demands total obedience to an oppressive ideology, condemns women to subservience, and marks unbelievers for murder. The other system is based on the conviction that freedom is the universal gift of Almighty God, and that liberty and justice light the path to peace.

This is the belief that gave birth to our nation. And in the long run, advancing this belief is the only practical way to protect our citizens. When people live in freedom, they do not willingly choose leaders who pursue campaigns of terror. When people have hope in the future, they will not cede their lives to violence and extremism. So around the world, America is promoting human liberty, human rights, and human dignity. We're standing with dissidents and young democracies, providing AIDS medicine to dying patients—to bring dying patients back to life, and sparing mothers and babies from malaria. And this great republic born alone in liberty is leading the world toward a new age when freedom belongs to all nations.

For eight years, we've also strived to expand opportunity and hope here at home. Across our country, students are rising to meet higher standards in public schools. A new Medicare prescription drug benefit is bringing peace of mind to seniors and the disabled. Every taxpayer pays lower income taxes. The addicted and suffering are finding new hope through faith-based programs. Vulnerable human life is better protected. Funding for our veterans has nearly doubled. America's air and water and lands are measurably cleaner. And the federal bench includes wise new members like Justice Sam Alito and Chief Justice John Roberts.

When challenges to our prosperity emerged, we rose to meet them. Facing the prospect of a financial collapse, we took decisive measures to safeguard our economy. These are very tough times for hardworking families, but the toll would be far worse if we had not acted. All Americans are in this together. And together, with determination and hard work, we will restore our economy to the path of growth. We will show the world once again the resilience of America's free enterprise system.

Like all who have held this office before me, I have experienced setbacks. There are things I would do differently if given the chance. Yet I've always acted with the best interests of our country in mind. I have followed my conscience and done what I thought was right. You may not agree with some of the tough decisions I have made. But I hope you can agree that I was willing to make the tough decisions.

The decades ahead will bring more hard choices for our country, and there are some guiding principles that should shape our course.

While our nation is safer than it was seven years ago, the gravest threat to our people remains another terrorist attack. Our enemies are patient, and determined to strike again. America did nothing to seek or deserve this conflict. But we have been given solemn responsibilities, and we must meet them. We must resist complacency. We must keep our resolve. And we must never let down our guard.

At the same time, we must continue to engage the world with confidence and clear purpose. In the face of threats from abroad, it can be tempting to seek comfort by turning inward. But we must reject isolationism and its companion, protectionism. Retreating behind our borders would only invite danger. In the 21st century, security and prosperity at home depend on the expansion of liberty abroad. If America does not lead the cause of freedom, that cause will not be led.

As we address these challenges—and others we cannot foresee tonight—America must maintain our moral clarity. I've often spoken to you about good and evil, and this has made some uncomfortable. But good and evil are present in this world, and between the two of them there can be no compromise. Murdering the innocent to advance an ideology is wrong every time, everywhere. Freeing people from oppression and despair is eternally right. This nation must continue to speak out for justice and truth. We must always be willing to act in their defense—and to advance the cause of peace.

President Thomas Jefferson once wrote, "I like the dreams of the future better than the history of the past." As I leave the house he occupied two centuries ago, I share that optimism. America is a young country, full of vitality, constantly growing and renewing itself. And even in the toughest times, we lift our eyes to the broad horizon ahead.

I have confidence in the promise of America because I know the character of our people. This is a nation that inspires immigrants to risk everything for the dream of freedom. This is a nation where citizens show calm in times of danger, and compassion in the face of suffering. We see examples of America's character all around us. And Laura and I have invited some of them to join us in the White House this evening.

We see America's character in Dr. Tony Recasner, a principal who opened a new charter school from the ruins of Hurricane Katrina. We see it in Julio Medina, a former inmate who leads a faith-based program to help prisoners returning to society. We've seen it in Staff Sergeant Aubrey McDade, who charged into an ambush in Iraq and rescued three of his fellow Marines.

We see America's character in Bill Krissoff—a surgeon from California. His son, Nathan—a Marine—gave his life in Iraq. When I met Dr. Krissoff and his family, he delivered some surprising news: He told me he wanted to join the Navy Medical Corps in honor of his son. This good man was 60 years old—18 years above the age limit. But his petition for a waiver was granted, and for the past year he has trained in battlefield medicine. Lieutenant Commander Krissoff could not be here tonight, because he will soon deploy to Iraq, where he will help save America's wounded warriors—and uphold the legacy of his fallen son.

In citizens like these, we see the best of our country—resilient and hopeful, caring and strong. These virtues give me an unshakable faith in America. We have faced danger and trial, and there's more ahead. But with the courage of our people and confidence in our ideals, this great nation will never tire, never falter, and never fail.

It has been the privilege of a lifetime to serve as your President.

There have been good days and tough days. But every day I have been inspired by the greatness of our country, and uplifted by the goodness of our people. I have been blessed to represent this nation we love. And I will always be honored to carry a title that means more to me than any other— citizen of the United States of America.

And so, my fellow Americans, for the final time: Good night. May God bless this house and our next President. And may God bless you and our wonderful country. Thank you.

Barack H. Obama

FAREWELL ADDRESS
TUESDAY, JANUARY 10, 2017

On January 10, 2017, on a cold Chicago night, President Obama gave his farewell address to an enthusiastic audience of admirers. Departing from the tradition of recent presidents in delivering a farewell address from the White House, Barack H. Obama chose McCormick Place in Chicago as the venue for his final speech.

IT'S GOOD TO BE HOME. My fellow Americans, Michelle and I have been so touched by all the well-wishes we've received over the past few weeks. But tonight it's my turn to say thanks. Whether we've seen eye-to-eye or rarely agreed at all, my conversations with you, the American people—in living rooms and schools; at farms and on factory floors; at diners and on distant outposts—are what have kept me honest, kept me inspired, and kept me going. Every day, I learned from you. You made me a better President, and you made me a better man.

I first came to Chicago when I was in my early twenties, still trying to figure out who I was; still searching for a purpose to my life. It was in neighborhoods not far from here where I began working with church groups in the shadows of closed steel mills. It was on these streets where I witnessed the power of faith, and the quiet dignity of working people in the face of struggle and loss. This is where I learned that change only happens when ordinary people get involved, get engaged, and come together to demand it.

After eight years as your President, I still believe that. And it's not just my belief. It's the beating heart of our American idea—our bold experiment in self-government.

It's the conviction that we are all created equal, endowed by our Creator with certain unalienable rights, among them life, liberty, and the pursuit of happiness.

It's the insistence that these rights, while self-evident, have never been self-executing; that We, the People, through the instrument of our democracy, can form a more perfect union.

This is the great gift our Founders gave us. The freedom to chase our individual dreams through our sweat, toil, and imagination—and the imperative to strive together as well, to achieve a greater good.

For 240 years, our nation's call to citizenship has given work and purpose to each new generation. It's what led patriots to choose republic over tyranny, pioneers to trek west, slaves to brave that makeshift railroad to freedom. It's what pulled immigrants and refugees across oceans and the Rio Grande, pushed women to reach for the ballot, powered workers to organize. It's why GIs gave their lives at Omaha Beach and Iwo Jima; Iraq and Afghanistan—and why men and women from Selma to Stonewall were prepared to give theirs as well.

So that's what we mean when we say America is exceptional. Not that our nation has been flawless from the start, but that we have shown the capacity to change, and make life better for those who follow.

Yes, our progress has been uneven. The work of democracy has always been hard, contentious and sometimes bloody. For every two steps forward, it often feels we take one step back. But the long sweep of America has been defined by forward motion, a constant widening of our founding creed to embrace all, and not just some.

If I had told you eight years ago that America would reverse a great recession, reboot our auto industry, and unleash the longest stretch of job creation in our history…if I had told you that we would open up a new chapter with the Cuban people, shut down Iran's nuclear weapons program without firing a shot, and take out the mastermind of 9/11…if I had told you that we would win marriage equality, and secure the right to health insurance for another 20 million of our fellow citizens—you might have said our sights were set a little too high.

But that's what we did. That's what you did. You were the change. You answered people's hopes, and because of you, by almost every measure, America is a better, stronger place than it was when we started.

In ten days, the world will witness a hallmark of our democracy: the peaceful transfer of power from one freely-elected president to the next. I committed to President-Elect Trump that my administration would ensure the smoothest possible transition, just as President Bush did for me. Because it's up to all of us to make sure our government can help us meet the many challenges we still face.

We have what we need to do so. After all, we remain the wealthiest, most powerful, and most respected nation on Earth. Our youth and drive, our diversity and openness, our boundless capacity for risk and reinvention mean that the future should be ours.

But that potential will be realized only if our democracy works. Only if our politics reflects the decency of the our people. Only if all of us, regardless of our party affiliation or particular interest, help restore the sense of common purpose that we so badly need right now.

That's what I want to focus on tonight—the state of our democracy.

Understand, democracy does not require uniformity. Our founders quarreled and compromised, and expected us to do the same. But they knew that democracy does require a basic sense of solidarity—the idea that for all our outward differences, we are all in this together; that we rise or fall as one.

There have been moments throughout our history that threatened to rupture that solidarity. The beginning of this century has been one of those times. A shrinking world, growing inequality; demographic change and the specter of terrorism—these forces haven't just tested our security and prosperity, but our democracy as well. And how we meet these challenges to our democracy will determine our ability to educate our kids, and create good jobs, and protect our homeland.

In other words, it will determine our future.

Our democracy won't work without a sense that everyone has economic opportunity. Today, the economy is growing again; wages, incomes, home values, and retirement accounts are rising again; poverty is falling again. The wealthy are paying a fairer share of taxes even as the stock market shatters records. The unemployment rate is near a ten-year low. The uninsured rate has never, ever been lower. Health care costs are rising at the slowest rate in fifty years. And if anyone can put together a plan that is demonstrably better than the improvements we've made to our health care system—that covers as many people at less cost—I will publicly support it.

That, after all, is why we serve—to make people's lives better, not worse.

But for all the real progress we've made, we know it's not enough. Our economy doesn't work as well or grow as fast when a few prosper at the expense of a growing middle class. But stark inequality is also corrosive to our democratic principles. While the top one percent has amassed a bigger share of wealth and income, too many families, in inner cities and rural counties, have been left behind—the laid-off factory worker; the waitress and health care worker who struggle to pay the bills—convinced that the game is fixed against them, that their government only serves the interests of the powerful—a recipe for more cynicism and polarization in our politics.

There are no quick fixes to this long-term trend. I agree that our trade should be fair and not just free. But the next wave of economic dislocation won't come from overseas. It will come from the relentless pace of automation that makes many good, middle-class jobs obsolete.

And so we must forge a new social compact—to guarantee all our kids the education they need; to give workers the power to unionize for better wages; to update the social safety net to reflect the way we live now and make more reforms to the tax code so corporations and individuals who reap the most from the new economy don't avoid their obligations to the country that's made their success possible. We can argue about how to best achieve these goals. But we can't be complacent about the goals themselves. For if we don't create opportunity for all people, the disaffection and division that has stalled our progress will only sharpen in years to come.

There's a second threat to our democracy—one as old as our nation itself. After my election, there was talk of a post-racial America. Such a vision, however well-intended, was never realistic. For race remains a potent and often divisive force in our society. I've lived long enough to know that race relations are better than they were ten, or twenty, or thirty years ago—you can see it not just in statistics, but in the attitudes of young Americans across the political spectrum.

But we're not where we need to be. All of us have more work to do. After all, if every economic issue is framed as a struggle between a hardworking white middle class and undeserving minorities, then workers of all shades will be left fighting for scraps while the wealthy withdraw further into their private enclaves. If we decline to invest in the children of immigrants, just because they don't look like us, we diminish the prospects of our own children—because those brown kids will represent a larger share of America's workforce. And our economy doesn't have to be a zero-sum game. Last year, incomes rose for all races, all age groups, for men and for women.

Going forward, we must uphold laws against discrimination—in hiring, in housing, in education and the criminal justice system. That's what our Constitution and highest ideals require. But laws alone won't be enough. Hearts must change. If our democracy is to work in this increasingly diverse nation, each one of us must try to heed the advice of one of the great characters in American fiction, Atticus Finch, who said "You never really understand a person until you consider things from his point of view…until you climb into his skin and walk around in it."

For blacks and other minorities, it means tying our own struggles for justice to the challenges that a lot of people in this country face—the refugee, the immigrant, the rural poor, the transgender American, and also the middle-aged white man who from the outside may seem like he's got all the advantages, but who's seen his world upended by economic, cultural, and technological change.

For white Americans, it means acknowledging that the effects of slavery and Jim Crow didn't suddenly vanish in the '60s; that when minority groups voice discontent, they're not just engaging in reverse racism or practicing political correctness; that when they wage peaceful protest, they're not demanding special treatment, but the equal treatment our Founders promised.

For native-born Americans, it means reminding ourselves that the stereotypes about immigrants today were said, almost word for word, about the Irish, Italians, and Poles. America wasn't weakened by the presence of these newcomers; they embraced this nation's creed, and it was strengthened.

So regardless of the station we occupy; we have to try harder; to start with the premise that each of our fellow citizens loves this country just as much as we do; that they value hard work and family like we do; that their children are just as curious and hopeful and worthy of love as our own.

None of this is easy. For too many of us, it's become safer to retreat into our own bubbles, whether in our neighborhoods or college campuses or places of worship or our social media feeds, surrounded by people who look like us and share the same political outlook and never challenge our assumptions. The rise of naked partisanship, increasing economic and regional stratification, the splintering of our media into a channel for every taste—all this makes this great sorting seem natural, even inevitable. And increasingly, we become so secure in our bubbles that we accept only information, whether true or not, that fits our opinions, instead of basing our opinions on the evidence that's out there.

This trend represents a third threat to our democracy. Politics is a battle of ideas; in the course of a healthy debate, we'll prioritize different goals, and the different means of reaching them. But without some common baseline of facts; without a willingness to admit new information, and concede that your opponent is making a fair point, and that science and reason matter, we'll keep talking past each other, making common ground and compromise impossible.

Isn't that part of what makes politics so dispiriting? How can elected officials rage about deficits when we propose to spend money on preschool for kids, but not when we're cutting taxes for corporations? How do we excuse ethical lapses in our own party, but pounce when the other party does the same thing? It's not just dishonest, this selective sorting of the facts; it's self-defeating. Because as my mother used to tell me, reality has a way of catching up with you.

Take the challenge of climate change. In just eight years, we've halved our dependence on foreign oil, doubled our renewable energy, and led the world to an agreement that has the promise to save this planet. But without bolder action, our children won't have time to debate the existence of climate change; they'll be busy dealing with its effects: environmental disasters, economic disruptions, and waves of climate refugees seeking sanctuary.

Now, we can and should argue about the best approach to the problem. But to simply deny the problem not only betrays future generations; it betrays the essential spirit of innovation and practical problem-solving that guided our Founders.

It's that spirit, born of the Enlightenment, that made us an economic powerhouse—the spirit that took flight at Kitty Hawk and Cape Canaveral; the spirit that cures disease and put a computer in every pocket.

It's that spirit—a faith in reason, and enterprise, and the primacy of right over might, that allowed us to resist the lure of fascism and tyranny during the Great Depression, and build a post-World War II order with other democracies, an order based not just on military power or national affiliations but on principles—the rule of law, human rights, freedoms of religion, speech, assembly, and an independent press.

That order is now being challenged—first by violent fanatics who claim to speak for Islam; more recently by autocrats in foreign capitals who see free markets, open democracies, and civil society itself as a threat to their power. The peril each poses to our democracy is more far-reaching than a car bomb or a missile. It represents the fear of change; the fear of people who look or speak or pray differently; a contempt for the rule of law that holds leaders accountable; an intolerance of dissent and free thought; a belief that the sword or the gun or the bomb or propaganda machine is the ultimate arbiter of what's true and what's right.

Because of the extraordinary courage of our men and women in uniform, and the intelligence officers, law enforcement, and diplomats who support them, no foreign terrorist organization has successfully planned and executed an attack on our homeland these past eight years; and although Boston and Orlando remind us of how dangerous radicalization can be, our law enforcement agencies are more effective and vigilant than ever. We've taken out tens of thousands of terrorists—including Osama bin Laden. The global coalition we're leading against ISIL has taken out their leaders, and taken away about half their territory. ISIL will be destroyed, and no one who threatens America will ever be safe. To all who serve, it has been the honor of my lifetime to be your Commander-in-Chief.

But protecting our way of life requires more than our military. Democracy can buckle when we give in to fear. So just as we, as citizens, must remain vigilant against external aggression, we must guard against a weakening of the values that make us who we are. That's why, for the past eight years, I've worked to put the fight against terrorism on a firm legal footing. That's why we've ended torture, worked to close Gitmo, and reform our laws governing surveillance to protect privacy and civil liberties. That's why I reject discrimination against Muslim Americans. That's why we cannot withdraw from global fights—to expand democracy, and human rights, women's rights, and LGBT rights—no matter how imperfect our efforts, no matter how expedient ignoring such values may seem. For the fight against extremism and intolerance and sectarianism are of a piece with the fight against authoritarianism and nationalist aggression. If the scope of freedom and respect for the rule of law shrinks around the world, the likelihood of war within and between nations increases, and our own freedoms will eventually be threatened.

So let's be vigilant, but not afraid. ISIL will try to kill innocent people. But they cannot defeat America unless we betray our Constitution and our principles in the fight. Rivals like Russia or China cannot match our influence around the world—unless we give up what we stand for, and turn ourselves into just another big country that bullies smaller neighbors.

Which brings me to my final point—our democracy is threatened whenever we take it for granted. All of us, regardless of party, should throw ourselves into the task of rebuilding our democratic institutions. When voting rates are some of the lowest among advanced democracies, we should make it easier, not harder, to vote. When trust in our institutions is low, we should reduce the corrosive influence of money in our politics, and insist on the principles of transparency and ethics in public service. When Congress is dysfunctional, we should draw our districts to encourage politicians to cater to common sense and not rigid extremes.

And all of this depends on our participation; on each of us accepting the responsibility of citizenship, regardless of which way the pendulum of power swings.

Our Constitution is a remarkable, beautiful gift. But it's really just a piece of parchment. It has no power on its own. We, the people, give it power—with our participation, and the choices we make. Whether or not we stand up for our freedoms. Whether or not we respect and enforce the rule of law. America is no fragile thing. But the gains of our long journey to freedom are not assured.

In his own farewell address, George Washington wrote that self-government is the underpinning of our safety, prosperity, and liberty, but "from different causes and from different quarters much pains will be taken...to weaken in your minds the conviction of this truth;" that we should preserve it with "jealous anxiety;" that we should reject "the first dawning of every attempt to alienate any portion of our country from the rest or to enfeeble the sacred ties" that make us one.

We weaken those ties when we allow our political dialogue to become so corrosive that people of good character are turned off from public service; so coarse with rancor that Americans with whom we disagree are not just misguided, but somehow malevolent. We weaken those ties when we define some of us as more American than others; when we write off the whole system as inevitably corrupt, and blame the leaders we elect without examining our own role in electing them.

It falls to each of us to be those anxious, jealous guardians of our democracy; to embrace the joyous task we've been given to continually try to improve this great nation of ours. Because for all our outward differences, we all share the same proud title: Citizen.

Ultimately, that's what our democracy demands. It needs you. Not just when there's an election, not just when your own narrow interest is at stake, but over the full span of a lifetime. If you're tired of arguing with strangers on the internet, try to talk with one in real life. If something needs fixing, lace up your shoes and do some organizing. If you're disappointed by your elected officials, grab a clipboard, get some signatures, and run for office yourself. Show up. Dive in. Persevere. Sometimes you'll win. Sometimes you'll lose. Presuming a reservoir of goodness in others can be a risk, and there will be times when the process disappoints you. But for those of us fortunate enough to have been a part of this work, to see it up close, let me tell you, it can energize and inspire. And more often than not, your faith in America—and in Americans—will be confirmed.

Mine sure has been. Over the course of these eight years, I've seen the hopeful faces of young graduates and our newest military officers. I've mourned with grieving families searching for answers, and found grace in a Charleston church. I've seen our scientists help a paralyzed man regain his sense of touch, and our wounded warriors walk again. I've seen our doctors and volunteers rebuild after earthquakes and stop pandemics in their tracks. I've seen the youngest of children remind us of our obligations to care for refugees, to work in peace, and above all to look out for each other.

That faith I placed all those years ago, not far from here, in the power of ordinary Americans to bring about change—that faith has been rewarded in ways I couldn't possibly have imagined. I hope yours has, too. Some of you here tonight or watching at home were there with us in 2004, in 2008, in 2012—and maybe you still can't believe we pulled this whole thing off.

You're not the only ones. Michelle—for the past twenty-five years, you've been not only my wife and mother of my children, but my best friend. You took on a role you didn't ask for and made it your own with grace and grit and style and good humor. You made the White House a place that belongs to everybody. And a new generation sets its sights higher because it has you as a role model. You've made me proud. You've made the country proud.

Malia and Sasha, under the strangest of circumstances, you have become two amazing young women, smart and beautiful, but more importantly, kind and thoughtful and full of passion. You wore the burden of years in the spotlight so easily. Of all that I've done in my life, I'm most proud to be your dad.

To Joe Biden, the scrappy kid from Scranton who became Delaware's favorite son: you were the first choice I made as a nominee, and the best. Not just because you have been a great Vice President, but because in the bargain, I gained a brother. We love you and Jill like family, and your friendship has been one of the great joys of our life.

To my remarkable staff: For eight years—and for some of you, a whole lot more—I've drawn from your energy, and tried to reflect back what you displayed every day: heart, and character, and idealism. I've watched you grow up, get married, have kids, and start incredible new journeys of your own. Even when times got tough and frustrating, you never let Washington get the better of you. The only thing that makes me prouder than all the good we've done is the thought of all the remarkable things you'll achieve from here.

And to all of you out there—every organizer who moved to an unfamiliar town and kind family who welcomed them in, every volunteer who knocked on doors, every young person who cast a ballot for the first time, every American who lived and breathed the hard work of change— you are the best supporters and organizers anyone could hope for, and I will forever be grateful. Because yes, you changed the world.

That's why I leave this stage tonight even more optimistic about this country than I was when we started. Because I know our work has not only helped so many Americans; it has inspired so many Americans— especially so many young people out there—to believe you can make a difference; to hitch your wagon to something bigger than yourselves. This generation coming up—unselfish, altruistic, creative, patriotic—I've seen you in every corner of the country. You believe in a fair, just, inclusive America; you know that constant change has been America's hallmark, something not to fear but to embrace, and you are willing to carry this hard work of democracy forward. You'll soon outnumber any of us, and I believe as a result that the future is in good hands.

My fellow Americans, it has been the honor of my life to serve you. I won't stop; in fact, I will be right there with you, as a citizen, for all my days that remain. For now, whether you're young or young at heart, I do have one final ask of you as your President—the same thing I asked when you took a chance on me eight years ago.

I am asking you to believe. Not in my ability to bring about change—but in yours.

I am asking you to hold fast to that faith written into our founding documents; that idea whispered by slaves and abolitionists; that spirit sung by immigrants and homesteaders and those who marched for justice; that creed reaffirmed by those who planted flags from foreign battlefields to the surface of the moon; a creed at the core of every American whose story is not yet written:

Yes We Can.

Yes We Did.

Yes We Can.

Thank you. God bless you. And may God continue to bless the United States of America.

CPSIA information can be obtained
at www.ICGtesting.com
Printed in the USA
LVOW12s1843060617
537131LV00002B/323/P